William Elliot Griffis

The Romance of Discovery

A thousand Years of exploration and the unveiling of Continents

William Elliot Griffis

The Romance of Discovery
A thousand Years of exploration and the unveiling of Continents

ISBN/EAN: 9783337066697

Printed in Europe, USA, Canada, Australia, Japan

Cover: Foto ©ninafisch / pixelio.de

More available books at **www.hansebooks.com**

THE ROMANCE OF DISCOVERY

THE NORSEMEN AND THEIR RAVEN PILOT.

THE ROMANCE OF DISCOVERY

*A Thousand Years of Exploration and
the Unveiling of Continents*

BY

WILLIAM ELLIOT GRIFFIS

MEMBER OF THE AMERICAN HISTORICAL ASSOCIATION
AUTHOR OF "THE MIKADO'S EMPIRE," "COREA, THE HERMIT NATION"
"BRAVE LITTLE HOLLAND," AND "SIR WILLIAM JOHNSON"

ILLUSTRATED BY

FRANK T. MERRILL

BOSTON
W. A. WILDE & COMPANY
25 BROMFIELD STREET

Dedicated

TO THE BOYS AND GIRLS

WHETHER BORN IN OR BROUGHT TO

The World's New and Better Europe

THE UNITED STATES OF AMERICA

PREFACE.

In this four hundredth anniversary year of John Cabot's landfall in North America, I have written, at the request of my publishers, this book entitled " The Romance of Discovery." It is intended to be the first of a series of three works in illustration of American history. The second volume will deal with the romance of colonization. The third will tell the story of American victories in war and diplomacy.

Strictly speaking, the discovery and exploration of America form but one of many phases in an ever-continuing movement of the Aryan race ; yet I have tried to show how America was reached and populated from the West, as well as from the East. I have not treated the achievement of Columbus as though it were a strange and unconnected episode, but rather as a link in a chain of events which issued in a knowledge to mankind of the Old as well as of the New World. I have tried to do justice to the various nationalities of Europe that took part in making known the continent between Europe and Asia. If I have given to Portugal, Holland, and Japan more credit than is usually bestowed by American authors, I have no other apology to make than the love of truth and fair play. Neither in this volume nor in any other history of the discovery of America, do our English ancestors figure very largely. Providence seems to have ordained that the Latin races should be pioneers, and that the English should enter into the labors of their southern brethren, in order that the best part of this continent might be won for the ideals of Christianized Germanic civilization. In the next volume, when the story of the colonies will be told, I trust that our English forefathers may receive the honors due them.

While following the best authorities, sincerely endeavoring to give true history and to exclude what is doubtful and unauthenticated, I have tried to show the powerful influence of romantic ideas, of myths and of fairy tales, upon human action, — in a word, the power of the world of imagination and fancy upon this world of toil, and especially upon the discovery and exploration of America. I trust that not a little personal familiarity, through travel, with our own and some of the other countries and the routes referred to, will but add to the value of this work.

My best thanks are due to my friend, William Nelson Noble, Esq., of Ithaca, whose criticisms and suggestions have been of service to me in the preparation of this work.

May this humble contribution to the history of the noblest of all lands nourish American patriotism, while hastening — though perhaps only as the raindrop hastens the harvest — that federation of the nations of the earth which is implied in our common Christianity.

W. E. G.

ITHACA ON CAYUGA LAKE, March 15, 1897.

TABLE OF CONTENTS.

———•◆•———

9

ILLUSTRATIONS.

11

THE ROMANCE OF DISCOVERY.

———∘∘⦂⦂∘∘———

IN geology, America is the old world; but in human history it is the new one. Before the other continents were shaped by the hand of God, He had already lifted up out of the waters the northern portion of America. Before ever a road was made by man, great natural highways had been trodden by animals whose existence preceded his own. Long before His creatures had found them out, the paths of God were in the sea, and His ways were upon the waters.

When first placed upon this globe, man was only a little child, who, as he grew up, but very gradually began to perceive the wisdom, love, and care of his Heavenly Father. Many thousands of years passed before he knew that there was one "gulf stream" in the Atlantic Ocean and another in the Pacific. Heat, light, and electricity are forces

which, ever since the creation, have been at all
times ready for the use of man; but it is only in
our own age that he has tamed and harnessed
them, even as he has tamed and harnessed the
animals that serve him, and it is but recently that
he has begun to do this.

The great prophet tells us that God did not
create the earth in vain; He formed it to be inhabited. But the question arises, Did men spread
over the earth like plants and animals? We have
been taught that the race originated in what is
called the "old world," — Asia. On that continent
written history began; and so Asia must be considered as being the old home of civilization.
Even so late as the fifteenth century, Europeans
had never dreamed of a "new world." It is true
that the Norwegians discovered Iceland in the
ninth century, and Greenland in the tenth; but
these islands were believed to be a part of the old
world, — Europe, Asia, and Africa. Indeed, neither
the suggestion of a "new world," nor the idea of
reaching Asia by sailing westward, could possibly
have entered the mind of man, until he had first
thought of the earth as being a globe, instead of
being flat like a table.

There had long been two natural passageways
from Asia to the "new world," both of which were
well used for many centuries before Europe had

acquired any knowledge of America. Let us consider them.

Glancing along the line of the Arctic Circle, either on a globe or a Mercator's chart, we perceive that there is a region of ice extending through Norway, Russia, Siberia, Alaska, British America, Greenland, and Iceland, over which one might make a journey around the top of the world. Travellers going eastward from Lapland could have reached Lapland again by land journeys, except where, in their skin boats, they were compelled to encounter the perils of the sea, crossing the narrow Behring Strait and the three water passages to Greenland, Iceland, and Norway. Along this route the "new world" was accessible to the inhabitants of the old one, who might reach it, going either east or west.

We are certain that in prehistoric times, journeys must have been made over this thoroughfare; for the Eskimo people, who lived in snow huts among the walrus and the polar bears, are found both in Asia and America.

There is another road to America which God made, most probably, before there was a man on the earth. This is a water-route along which one might easily have journeyed, even in the childhood days of the race, when the boatman had no compass, chart, or sextant. Although there were no

lighthouses to guide his course, there were great
landmarks pointing the directions of going and
coming. We shall also find that both the winds
and currents were most favorable for a trip eastward to America. Very curiously, this ocean pathway is along a line of earthquakes, and of volcanoes
which often furnish light at night and smoke by
day, so that pillars of fire and of cloud have guided
wanderers in the wilderness ocean, from the old
seats of nations to the lonely continent, America.
Man's first need is for food, then for clothing and
shelter. Along this route the traveller can find
plenty to eat, since nature has established, as it
were, restaurants at stations along the way. Moreover, shelter has been provided for him; while
all sorts of material for clothing, both that
which grows out of the ground and that which
grows on the backs of animals, have been ever
at hand.

Thus the Power, or the Providence, that made
and furnished this great and wonderful highway
was ever inviting the peoples of the old world to
discover the new lands toward the sunrise. He
not only made the ocean canal, but He beckoned
onward. Let us look at this remarkable sea-road.

In the Pacific Ocean, between the Tropic of
Cancer and Micronesia, there is a great current
which flows up from the equator (where, under the

vertical rays of the sun, the water almost boils), and which, moving for the most part westward, meets the great hot drifts coming up past Borneo and the Philippines. Thus both streams form a great, deep blue river in the sea, which, rushing like a mill race, scours the front of Formosa and the long chain of Japanese Islands. It then crosses eastward toward the Aleutian Islands, and, flowing down to Vancouver, passes along the whole western front of the United States, Mexico, and Central America. It is a curious fact that in this warm and indigo-blue stream anything that can float will move over a great circle of the earth.

Moreover, all the way from the Malay Archipelago to Vancouver, the water is comparatively shallow. Consequently it is a great feeding ground for fish and other marine creatures which supply nourishment to man, and attract from the interior highlands down to the coast, such other animals as also prey upon this sea-food. Even a savage boy, without much trouble, might easily make a journey along this ocean canal, because he would always have landmarks to guide his course; for all along there are thousands of islands full of inlets and harbors, which are like stepping-stones and may be used for resting-places. The many-colored waters indicate, like a barometer, the condition of the weather and furnish daily probabilities. Even the

c

fishes and the birds are good pilots, and one need rarely be troubled with any terrors of the lonely deep.

Thus, along a great circle of the earth, there is a well-marked ocean pathway, illumined by light-giving volcanoes, provided with the proper winds to bend the sail and furnish motor power, having a temperature substantially uniform along the whole route, and abundantly supplied with food. This great, warm stream, the " Nile of the Pacific," de-posits over the beds of landlocked areas, tropical silt and lower forms of marine creatures which feed fish and animals, thus contributing to the life of man. The best fishing-grounds of the world are in this ocean river, along which, as we shall see, America received most of its inhabitants who came from Asia.

There is this great difference between the North Atlantic and the North Pacific. To navigate the ocean between America and Europe, one must sail boldly out from sight of land without mountain peaks or islands to guide his course. In the far north, there is only the little Faroe Island group between Iceland and Norway. Further south there is nothing; and the route from continent to conti-nent shows only unbroken water. What wonder that on the ancient maps the Atlantic Ocean was indicated as being a great " Sea of Darkness "?

What wonder that no American Indian ever drifted away to Europe?

It is otherwise in the Pacific Ocean, which is spotted all over with islands, especially in the north and south. Above and below the Equator is a great archipelago. Along the Tropic of Cancer are the Hawaiian and other islands in mid-ocean, and the Japanese and Philippine islands are nearer the continent. In the northern Pacific are the Kuriles, — well called "the smokers," — with the Aleutian Islands not far off, and then Alaska.

Let us now look at these Asians who became the first Americans, whom the sailors from Norway called "Skralligs," and the discoverer from Italy named "Indians."

CHAPTER II.

THERE are many ways of learning history. We read it not only from written documents, monuments, and coins, but also from the science of ethnology, from geological relics, from language, and from what is written on the body of man. We know that civilization always springs up along the water, in warm river valleys, such as those of the Nile, Euphrates, Tigris, Ganges, and Yang-tse. While the people having writing and books — the Egyptians, Assyrians, Hindoos, and Chinese — were growing into nations, there was a human stream of the dark-skinned races, reddish, brown, and yellow, moving along nature's oldest highway from Asia into America. One set of peoples was of the northern or Eskimo type, like their cousins in Siberia. Another set had red skins, like the copper-colored Formosan head-hunters of to-day.

When southern Europeans first reached the West Indies in the fifteenth century, the Eskimos occupied the region just below and inside the Arctic Circle. The various Indian tribes roaming over

what is now the United States, north and east,
seemed to have developed in and migrated from
the valley of the Columbia River. In the Mississippi valley were the buffalo hunters, who lived
and migrated with these animals. In the east, the
Iroquois and Algonquins lived on fish and deer,
and had maize lands. In what is now the southwest of the United States and Mexico, there was a
great group of tribes living in the dry regions. In
South America, the home of mighty forests as large
as Europe, were many tribes of Indians. In Peru
they had developed something like civilization.

Although the inhabitants of the whole continent
of America seem, on first view, so different, and
although there were one hundred and twenty separate families of languages, yet all the tribes in
America except the Eskimos were much alike in
one great social principle. Marriage must be
inside the tribe and descent remain in the female
line. There were many handicrafts and cunning
devices of hunter, fisherman, warrior, farmer, or
weaver; but nothing absolutely new was invented
on this continent. Every one of the aboriginal
American arts — of industry, of war, and of ornament — can be matched in Asia, Oceanica, or Europe. All the myths and folklore of the Indians
point to their origin in the northwest and to Asia
beyond.

How numerous the inhabitants of America were in 1492, we do not know, but we are certain that the population was densest where food was plentiful and readily obtained, and in regions of country where paths and communications were easy and natural. Great areas of the continent, some of them larger than Europe, were almost wholly uninhabited by man. In British America there is a forest seventeen hundred miles long from east to west, and a thousand miles wide from north to south. This was not used or traversed by the red men until game grew scarce in the Hudson's Bay region, when trappers were compelled to go farther afield for flesh or furs. Another stretch of timber land covers a large part of the state of Washington and British Columbia. In the valley of the Amazon River, we are in darkest South America. The thicket, covering much of northern Brazil and the eastern portions of those countries between Brazil and the Pacific, is twenty-one hundred miles long by thirteen hundred miles wide. Very few people dwelt in these regions.

So also in the desert of Nevada, and in the great dry and thirsty lands of Arizona, New Mexico, and Texas, but few human beings could exist away from the river valleys. As a rule, the mountains, the thick forests, and the waterless regions were but slightly used or occupied. We may say at once, that over a large portion of the Americas, the only human habitations were those of hunters and occasional wanderers. The mass of the aborigines gathered along the watercourses, at the river mouths on the seacoast, and in fertile valleys; in a word, where they could get food, find good trails on land, and secure water-ways for their canoes.

Seeking food and making war were the chief occupations of the first Americans, who were mostly of the stone age. Their land journeys were on foot. The Eskimos and Canadian Indians had dogs to pull their sleds. Down in Peru they used a little camel, the llama, but the chief means of transportation were the human back and legs. Even in their savage state, men and women had many wants. The fishermen living near the sea-shore needed what the hunters dwelling in the interior could furnish. Thus barter grew up. The seacoast tribes furnished salt, dried clams, oysters, and fish, shells for wampum and ornament; while the interior tribes supplied meat, skins, flint arrow-heads, pipe-stone, and tobacco. The women did the drudgery of tilling the fields, cooking, and housekeeping, besides rearing the children; while the men made weapons and tools, hunted, fished, and fought.

Who built the mounds, we do not know, nor can

we tell whether the mound-builders were a race
separate from and previous to the red Indians; or,
whether, as is most probable, they were the same
people.   But centuries before any white man from
Europe saw America, there was a lively commerce
between these mound-builders; for among their
remains we find obsidian knives from Mexico and
the Yellow Stone Park, mica from North Carolina,
gold, silver, meteoric iron, and shells, from the Gulf
of Mexico.   Indian commerce in its total bulk was
enormous.   In many old quarries we find the abandoned workshops of these ancient artificers, and
hard by the unnoticed relics along old streams, once
dammed by beavers, we see their trapping grounds.

The industries of the Americans were varied and
remarkable.   The introduction of new weapons
from Europe, like firearms, axes, and iron arrow-
heads, destroyed the old Indian trades and workshops, just as steam and improved machinery,
applied to weaving in England, have left the ruins
of many water-power mills along the inland streams.
European tools, clothing, money, and hundreds of
other things which the red men wanted, threw out
of employment thousands of expert native workmen
and left the old workshops, in the quarries, the forest, and the seashore, deserted and useless.   In
prehistoric times, before white men destroyed the
old native crafts, some of the Indian specialists

were expert bow-makers; others chipped arrow-
heads. One man made spear-points or chisels,
another scrapers, and still others dishes or jewellery.
The fingers of some squaws were nimble in mould-
ing earthen vessels, others were expert in weaving
and embroidering, while still others gathered up
shells in summer and strung them into wampum
during the winter. The younger and stronger men
became famous as warriors or hunters and rose to
be chiefs. There was almost as much division of
labor and consequent expertness in some tribes as
there is in modern civilized life.

Wherever groups of Indians who were able to do
something more than hunt or fish, could plant and
raise crops and store food away and engage in traffic, there a higher state of civilization was reached.
In the long run, the farmer is always able to excel
the mere hunter. In Peru the Indians knew how
to make hard metal tools and build stone fortresses,
and possessed well-laid-out cities. They wove cloth,
made wonderful gold ornaments, cut statues, and had
a powerful military organization. In Mexico and
in Peru, also, they irrigated their lands. They were
expert in digging canals, in making dikes, and in
chiselling and polishing hard stone. In Arizona
they had towns and fortresses on the tops of rocks,
with dwellings hollowed out in the cliffs, and they
had made some progress in the arts. In New

York, between the Niagara and the Hudson, the
five Iroquois tribes had great farms of corn, beans,
squashes, and pumpkins, and could store up large
quantities of food. They built long houses of timber and bark, each of which held a number of families. They had well-situated and fortified towns,
while their commerce was highly developed. Their
confederacy was a remarkable political structure,
and there were among them not only thousands of
fierce warriors, but many leaders skilled in statecraft and diplomacy.

So it was not an empty wilderness which the
Norsemen or Columbus were to discover, but a
land populated with millions of human beings,
whose social life, languages, political and military
methods, arms and architecture, commerce and
trade, were well worth the study of the new-comers
from Europe. They even had some art in communi-
cating ideas and various methods of handing down
tradition. The native Americans were probably as
religious in their way as the Europeans who conquered them were in theirs. The men of the stone
age had already discovered and occupied this continent long before the invaders from across the
Atlantic appeared with iron, agriculture, writing,
and a superior religion.

As had already happened on a smaller scale in
India, China, Japan, and other countries, so here in

America the same thing took place and the same story may be told again. It was one of discovery, exploration, colonization, conquest, with much cruelty on the side of the conquerors and some improvement of the aborigines. In most portions the amalgamation of conqueror and conquered followed. In others the ancient inhabitants were first enslaved and then, partially or wholly, converted to the imported faith. It was a mutual discovery which the Americans and Europeans made of each other; and it is more than probable that they who had more light did not act with any more reason or righteousness. How the different nations who discovered the aborigines treated them, — the one for the most part preserving and the other destroying, — we shall learn in the course of our three separate narratives, "The Romance of Discovery," "The Romance of Colonization," and "The Romance of Conquest."

The first of these North American people ever seen by Europeans were called "Skralligs," as we shall see.

CHAPTER III.

UP in the far north of Europe, in the high latitudes where the summer days are very long, often with eighteen or twenty hours of sun or twilight, but where the winter days are very short, live the hardy Scandinavians. They fill all the region between the Baltic and the North Seas, and between the Gulf of Bothnia and the Atlantic Ocean. Theirs is a great mountain land full of dark and gloomy forests, with uncounted lakes and streams which never dry up, because fed by the endless snows and ice.

Along the shore of Norway, from the North Cape, where one can see the summer sun at midnight, down to "the naze," or nose, runs a coast which is walled with mountains, but pierced all along with fiords. These are deep narrow cracks in the earth's crust, full of water, with many a cove and beach, where boats can be built and launched, and where hardy men and women are reared. Together with the fiords are numberless islands, rich in meat and eggs, and birds and fish. Here is situated one of

28

nature's great schools for the training of brave and
hardy sailors.

In this great region of the Norsemen, which in-
cludes Denmark, Sweden, and Norway, has long
lived a fair-haired, blue-eyed race; hardy, vigorous,
and daring, fond of the sea, and not afraid of its
waves or storms. How long these blond folks have
lived here, cannot be reckoned. Ages ago their
ancestors dwelt among these same rocks and waters.
They did not become Christians until about the
time of Christianity's millennial year. While in the
warm and rich region of the Mediterranean, great
cathedrals and splendid edifices in stone rose to the
glory of God in Christ, and the stories of Bethlehem,
of Nazareth, of Jerusalem, and of Calvary were familiar in every household, these people in the far
north were still mostly pagans. Some tribes of
them, marching overland, but oftener rowing out in
their barges, and sailing in their ships, had reached
the shores of Netherlands, Great Britain, France,
and Germany. Besides war and slaughter, battle
and burning, they had made settlements. Some
had even gone to the Mediterranean Sea and sailed
as far as Constantinople. Coming back, they told
of the wonders of the warm lands where oranges,
lemons, and olives grew.

Fierce and bloody were these pagan Norsemen
who enjoyed nothing more than a raid upon French

or Dutch market towns, many a one of which they
left in ashes. They also liked to go into Christian
churches and defile or burn the sacred emblems,
of whose meaning they knew nothing. For centuries, Christian people kneeling on their church floors
prayed every Sunday in their litany, "From the fury
of the Norsemen, good Lord, deliver us." When
the English caught the robbers, Dane or Norse,
they used to skin them alive and nail their hides
to the church doors. In the Netherlands they cut
off their heads on the wet sea-beach.

Yes, these men, ancestors of many of us, were
pagans. They had a mythology which explained
to them the world and creation. It did not tell of
a garden of Eden, so warm that a man and his wife
could live without clothing and not feel cold, but of
an original northern chaos, or rather of two worlds.
In one, there were ice-cold streams, icebergs, and
snow crystals. In the other, which was bright and
hot, sat a guardian deity with a flaming sword.
When the two worlds met in conflict, and the sparks
and the frost vapor came together, large drops tric-
kled down. These took the form of an immense
giant named Ymer, and of a great cow named Aud-
humbla. The cow nourished the mighty giant and
fed herself by licking the salty frost crystals on the
rocks. After three days a man named Bure was
produced, and there being a giantess named Bestla,

three sons were born. These, when they grew up,
slew the giant Ymer, and out of his dead body they
made the present world.

So, to the boys and girls who grew up in the
old Norse world, the earth was the giant's flesh,
the ocean was his blood, the rocks were his bones,
the trees of the forest were his hairs, the great,
round, vaulted sky was his skull, and the clouds
were his brains. However, the giants had not all
died, and there were wars between them and the
men.

Dwarfs and elves lived on the earth, while beneath
it were the inhabitants of the lower world. The
gods and the men were friends, but the giants and
the underworld people were the enemies of both
gods and men.

Wonderful is the Norse mythology, which these
first discoverers of the Faroe Islands and Iceland
believed. Curiously enough, showing how mythology is true to nature, of all the giants, Ægir, the
ruler of the sea, is the wealthiest. So rich indeed
is he, that he once entertained all the gods in his
magnificent hall in grand style. It was over the
seas of Ægir that the hardy Norseman rowed and
sailed to reach the rich lands of the South, and seize
the wealth of towns and churches. The giant's blood,
as they called the ocean, gave them food, and ever
tempted them to adventure and booty.

One of these Northmen discovered Greenland, but did not name it. Later, in the year 982, Erik the Red, who had been banished there from Iceland, gave an example to all land agents and speculators, who wish to sell lands, whether valuable or worthless, by writing an attractive advertisement. Erik named this gray and white country of rock, ice, and polar bears, Greenland, in order to attract colonists.

The Norwegians were the first Europeans to see and dwell in America. In their days there was no compass, chart, sextant, or chronometer. The splendid equipments of modern ships and the science of navigation based on mathematics, were unknown; but there were bold hearts, iron-like muscles, hardy bodies, and strong wills. God's lights in the skies were theirs. The sun, rising and setting every day, gave them true direction east and west, — a path of golden light, — as they thought, over the blood of Ymer. At night the glorious stars, set into the round skull of the world-giant, shed their mild radiance. How easy to sail straight westward!

No wonder that Iceland was early discovered, colonized, and made one of the homes of these blond and blue-eyed people. No wonder, either, that Greenland was so early known and visited that when the South Europeans learned geography from the Arabs and began to think of the matter, they considered Greenland to be a part of the old world, because it belonged to European people.

But what happened, when clouds hid sun and star, when mist and fog covered the surface of the ocean, when adverse winds blew and terrible currents drove the ships out of their courses, and storms howled and roared, sending rain, sleet, and ice into the faces and over the bodies of the hardy mariners? Then, to the Norsemen's fancy, the brains of Ymer were blowing about, hiding the light and the land. Without chart or compass, what could these vikings — men of the viks or bays, yet true kings of the sea — do?

In the earlier world, as among the Indians of the forest to-day, the average man lived nearer to the beasts and birds. The creatures of fin, fur, feather, and hoof were like companions. The man often lived under the same roof with his horses, cows, and pet birds, and when he died, he wanted them buried with him. He understood the language, motions, and powers of the brutes better than does the civilized man in our time. So, when the Norseman sailed far from land, he took a pilot with him. This pilot was black and feathered. It was a raven. Before ever he had heard of Father Noah and his ark, he took this ancient friend of man, yet so much feared, in his ship with him. Far out at sea, beyond the roar of breakers, or the scent of smoke or trees, or even amid wintry gales and cloud-covered skies, or in fog or mist, the raven was set free. While in sight, its course was watched with intense straining eyes. If the bird came back, then land was not near. If it did not return, the men rowed with all speed in the direction of its flight, and soon they landed on some shore.

Robert Browning, the poet, once wrote : —

"God guides me and the bird."

In the story of Ararat, of the Norseman, and of the first Italian in America, "our little brothers of the air," with wisdom taught them by the Almighty, found for Noah, for Leif, and for Columbus, the path to land.

CHAPTER IV.

IT was in A.D. 986 that Bjarne, an Icelander, while on his way to Greenland with Erik the Red, to help make a settlement in the new country, had a most wonderful adventure. Three days after they had left Iceland the wind blew from the north, and continued during several days, driving them far southward and into a fog. When at length the sun appeared, so that they could discover east and west, and north and south, they found land along the horizon, but no part of it corresponded with Greenland. On this new and strange shore they saw no high mountains, but only wooded hills. Being so far out of their course, they did not venture to leave their ship, but, turning round, sailed northward and finally reached Greenland, having twice, in the meanwhile, sighted land on the left.

What could this new land have been, if not some part of northeastern America? The story of Bjarne's adventure is told in the Sagas, which are

35

famous old Norwegian books of poetry. It is believed by some, that Bjarne first saw some part of
Maine or Massachusetts, then Nova Scotia, and then
Newfoundland. A few years later Bjarne came to
Norway and told of his discovery. Leif Erikson,
who heard him, was mightily excited, and wanted
to see that new land again. So he bought Bjarne's
ship, and gathered thirty-five hardy men to go out
and look upon these new lands.

In the same kind of stoutly ribbed, undecked
boats, such as have been dug up occasionally out of
the old vikings' graves, let us imagine Leif Erikson
and his crew setting out from Norway in the year
A.D. 1000. Leif is a hardy Icelander, thirty years
of age. He is not a pagan, but has become a
Christian; for the bright light of the new religion
is breaking over the dark forests of Norway, and
already the harper and minstrels are singing songs
in the king's court, about Bethlehem and its mes-
sage of peace.

Like so many later ones, this is a missionary
expedition. King Olaf wants Leif to go to Greenland, and preach the story of Christ and the Cross
to the natives. Without religion, America would
never have been discovered by Norse, Spaniard, or
Italian. This is the first motive that launches the
ship and drives it westward; but there is also
another which appeals to the spirit of daring and

adventure, and by this motive the hardy young man Leif is impelled.

We can imagine his starting. A Norse boat at that time was heavily built, with long planks or strips of wood riveted with iron and braced with knee-timbers, stoutly tied with thongs. In the strong gunwales, the oar locks were solid and part of the wood. The huge prow rose up in the form of a dragon, or was shaped like the head of a cow. The captain stood on a platform near the bow, for there was no deck. The keel and swelling sides were so arranged that when run on shore the boat could be covered over and used as a house. In time of favorable winds, the seats of the rowers were empty, and their battle shields hung along the gunwales. Instead of a high stern-post and rudder, there was on the right, near the end, a long and wide oar, — the "steer-board," from whence we get our word "star-board." On a fair day their short and small flags would flutter at the mast-head. Anciently, these had pictures of the raven or dragon on them. Probably, since Leif was a Christian, there would be at the top of the mast, and above its one big sail, the figure of the cross, which might also be on its pennon. Perhaps he carried a cage of ravens as winged pilots.

The comforts of life could not have been very numerous on such a craft. Their food, of the

roughest kind, was generally eaten uncooked.
When the breeze was stiff behind, they need not
row; but they had to toil all day at the oar when
the wind was not favorable. They were constantly
wet in stormy weather. In winter, with beards
hung with icicles or coated with rime, sleet on
their eyebrows and hair, and ice covering their
clothes and the boat side, their hardships were such
as only the strongest men could endure. Nevertheless, in the year of the Columbian Exposition at
Chicago, in 1893, a party of hardy young Norwegians crossed the Atlantic in a craft built on the
model of an ancient viking's ship.

The Sagas tell us that Leif found the coast seen
by Bjarne far to the south of Greenland. The
first landfall, which was probably Newfoundland, he
named the Country of Slates, or of flat stones. The
second, which was probably Nova Scotia, he called
Woodland. Finally, he reached some part of the
continent to the southwest, which might have
been the valley of the Charles River, near Boston;
or, possibly, Rhode Island, which place he named
Vineland, or Wine Land.

Here he settled and spent the winter. On account of the great number of wild grapes growing
there, he gave the country its name. The Sagas
go on to tell us about the grain, the grapes, and
the fish, as well as about the natives, who do not

seem to have been very friendly. These "Skralligs" were probably not Eskimos, but red Indians.

In the springtime, when the days began to be
long, and the great features of the sky and landmarks could be easily distinguished, Leif made his
voyage homeward. On the way he was able to
rescue fifteen men from shipwreck, and so was
called Leif the Lucky. When his father died in
Greenland, he became the chief of the colony, and
lived until A.D. 1021.

Leif had a brother named Thorvald. This man
started off in a single ship, and with his people
lived three winters in Vineland, making explorations
meanwhile south and north. From first to last
women have had a great deal to do with the making of America. It was a Norse woman who now
proposed a colony in Vineland, instead of a camp.
In the year 1006 a Norwegian named Thorfinn
arrived in Greenland. He married a widow named
Gudrid, and she induced him to sail with his ships
to Vineland, and make permanent dwelling there.
They took with them cattle and other things necessary for their homes. During the first winter,
which was very severe, a son was born of the couple
and named Snorre. From this child, who first
saw light in the yet unnamed America, the great
Danish sculptor Thorvaldsen claimed descent. In
the springtime they moved to the spot where Leif

Erikson had spent the winter. After three years Thorfinn, with part of his colonists, returned to Greenland.

After that, trading voyages were common between Greenland and Vineland. The ships brought timber to Greenland, where it was very much needed for the building of Christian churches. One of the missionary bishops of Greenland, Erik Upsi, went to Vineland in 1121. The accounts in the Sagas of the voyagers are very full of detail, but are not of the kind that we should like to have, so as to prove absolutely that the Norsemen really occupied a part of what is now the United States.

These men were hardy sailors, but not scholars, prophets, or scientific men. They tell of killing bears, of finding eggs when they were hungry, of burying their chief who was slain in battle, of a rock shaped like a ship's keel, of broad and flat-faced natives who wanted to sell furs, of the beaches where they hauled up their ships, and of the strong tides and currents, — just the things that do most interest sailors. We even learn what articles of commerce they sought and carried away.

Voyages to Vineland continued until that awful event in the history of Norway which broke the spirit of the Norsemen, and made them the quiet and unadventurous people which they continued to be from the time of Columbus until the modern

revival of marine enterprise under Nordenskjöld,
who found the Northeast Passage, and sailed over
the north of Asia to Japan in 1879, and Nansen,
who, in 1895, nearly reached the North Pole. The
event which stopped further exploration and commerce with America was the awful plague called
the Black Death. It broke out at the beginning
of the second quarter of the fourteenth century, and
until A.D. 1350 ravaged the country, depopulating
the valleys and seacoasts, and sweeping off one
third of the nation. The last record of a Norse
ship that went to Vineland after timber is of A.D.
1347. From that time forth a great fog, such as
blots out the sight of sky and land from the sailor,
falls upon history, and we see no more of the hardy
Norsemen in North American waters.

It is yet uncertain whether the Norsemen discovered America precisely as their friends and
admirers, led by Professor Eben Horsford, think
they did. We cannot tell exactly where the Norsemen had their settlement, although the Sagas seem
reasonably clear on the general subject. Iceland's
oldest historian, Ari, as early as 1130, speaks of the
discovery of Vineland. He got his information
from his uncle, who, when a boy, had lived in
Greenland. There he learned about the discoveries from an old man, who had himself accompanied Erik the Red from Iceland in 986, and had

seen Leif Erikson when he came back from Vineland. From Ari the Wise came the later accounts
of the discovery of Vineland. One account was
got by a bishop from a peasant on Flatty Island,
off the west coast of Iceland, and in the fourteenth
century this islander's story was put into writing.

Whether Columbus learned about America from
the Scandinavian sailors whom he must have met
at the ports, or from Norse books and writings, we
cannot tell; but this we do know:

(1) That the Pope and other foreign potentates
in the thirteenth century sought the friendship of
Haakon, King of Norway, "in view of his power
and experience on the sea."

(2) That Adam of Bremen, writing late in the
eleventh century, makes distinct mention of the
regions which had been discovered by the Norsemen. After describing Iceland and Greenland, he
tells us that the nephew of Canute the Great "men-
tioned another land which had been discovered in
this ocean [the Atlantic] which is called Vineland,
because the vine producing excellent wine grows
there spontaneously, and corn grows there abundantly without being sown. This we know not
from fabulous conjecture, but from positive state-
ments of the Danes." It may have been that
Columbus saw this book, which was written in Latin
and circulated throughout Europe. Columbus vis-

ited Iceland in February, 1477, and could easily have heard about the lands discovered by Leif Erikson.

(3) That Gudrid, the widow of Thorfinn, after her return to Norway, made a pilgrimage to Rome, where she was well received. It would be strange indeed if her tongue had been silent about her wonderful experiences.

Many still believe it was in the region back of Boston and in the basin of the Charles River that the Norsemen lived, traded and fought the Skralligs or savage natives, and that the traditional and almost mythical city of Norumbega lay there. Indeed, my friend, the late Professor Eben Horsford, was so confident that this was the place described in the Sagas that he bought several acres of land near Malden, Mass., and there erected a memorial to the Norse discoverers. This is a handsome tower of boulders and pebbles, having upon its front a polished granite tablet giving a translation of the passages from the Sagas which show what the Norsemen collected and exported. These were Masur-wood, or burls, fish, furs, and agricultural products. He thought that the name Norumbega was only the Indian's corruption of Norveger (Norway). Near Watertown, Professor Horsford believed he found docks, dams, walls, basins, terraced places of assembly, and at Malden, a fort. Whatever we may believe, it is certain that the

Norsemen were the pathfinders for Columbus and the pioneers of later discoveries. Before their time, all the other peoples of Europe practised navigation only by moving along the shore with landmarks in view. The idea of striking out into the unmarked and pathless ocean, and through the imagined "sea of darkness," was unknown to the more southern European peoples, and it was never attempted by them until after the Northmen had done it. On the contrary, the Norwegians, who probably invented, or re-invented the keel, struck boldly out of sight of land with nothing but the great lights of heaven to guide, and with only the ravens for their pilots — even as these had helped Elijah and directed Noah before their time. Thus as perfectly as in a mathematical demonstration, they proved the possibility of navigating the deep and unmarked ocean. It is not likely that in the future progress of research, the modest honors of the Norsemen, in the history of discovery, will ever be taken from them.

CHAPTER V.

WE think it a great thing that between the Norsemen, Columbus, Cabot, and Amerigo Vespucci, America was discovered; but it was almost as wonderful that the old world itself was found out. It required many hundreds of years to learn the boundaries and form of the old world of Europe, Asia, Africa, and Australia.

While the Norsemen were rowing their galleys about the coasts of northern and southern Europe, and even driving their keels westward in deep-sea navigation, those Asiatic Norsemen, the Japanese, were finding out their far eastern world. They were brave men, not afraid to leave the shore. During the twelfth and thirteenth centuries, their sailors roamed southward into the Riu Kiu archipelago and to Formosa, which they conquered. At the same time their daring pirates and navigators were scouring the seas and coasts north, south, and west. Landing in Tartary, Korea, and China, these Oriental brown men struck the same terror among the peoples of these countries as the Occi-

dental blonds did among Europeans. To this
day, the name and the dread of the Japanese are
upon all the coast peoples from Kamtchatka to
Siam and the Philippines. The mothers of Chinese and Korean children still scare their naughty
boys and girls by the name of the "Wo-jin," or
Japanese. In the course of centuries, especially
during that very long peace, in Tycoon times,
from the days of the Pilgrims to those of Commodore Perry, these exploits of the ancient and mediæval Japanese buccaneers and raiders became fairy
tales, like that of "Jack the Giant-Killer." This
folk-lore is still told not only in Japanese, but
in other languages, though with many a curious
variation.

The Japanese had something to do not only with
the discovery of America, but also with the populat-
ing and making of it. Ages ago they noticed the
dark blue river of warm water flowing northward in
the ocean's mass, and they named it Kuro Shiwo
or the Black Stream. Into this indigo-blue current,
during centuries upon centuries, Japanese fishermen
and sailors, often with their wives and children, have
been caught in storms and driven out to sea. Help-
less in the Black Stream, they have drifted along,
often to lingering death by thirst or starvation, but
often also to new life in a new world. Landing on
the Aleutian Islands, Alaska, British America or

California, they have intermixed with the natives and their names have been lost, though many of their words survive.

All this is a matter not of mere guess, but of Japanese tradition and history, and the actual record of hundreds of cases. Many of those picked up at sea, thousands of miles from Japan, I have known personally. Japanese coins and other objects have been often found at many points along the Pacific American coast. Not a few Japanese words are easily recognized in the speech of the northwestern coast Indians. Without any doubt, a notable part of the population of North America has come from that Japanese archipelago which, since 1894, extends from the Philippines to Kamtchatka. Every year in our century, Japanese and other waifs, living or dead, have been noted or rescued at sea. In the days before general European navigation, they drifted helplessly to ruin or were stranded on the coast which curves all the way round from Nippon to Mexico.

It is remarkable that both the great ocean currents were discovered by Americans. Dr. Benjamin Franklin, in crossing the Atlantic, noticed the seam between the warm and cold water and the difference in color, and called the attention of the sailors to it. The Pacific Stream, the Black Current of the Japanese, was first discovered, that is, scientifically studied, located, explained, and mapped by a brilliant American naval officer, Captain Silas Bent, who visited Japan with Captain Glynn in 1850, and with Commodore M. C. Perry in 1853-54.

There have been some who think that the Chinese also knew about America, but the book about Fu-san, or Fusang, is probably nothing more than a description by some Chinese traveller of Fu-san in Korea, and does not concern America. Nevertheless, it is quite probable that not a few Chinese sailors have drifted up to Kuro Shiwo, and landed on the shores of America. For ages the Japanese have had notions, such as we find in romances and fairy tales, about Fusang (or Fuso) and Horai, which might have been in America, if anywhere. Many other myths, such as the Amazon's country, or island inhabited only by women, the philosopher's stone, the elixir of life, and various sorts of Utopias, were common in the Mikado's empire. No Japanese or Chinese ever "discovered" America in any other way than that of Madoc, the Welshman, that is, in imagination, or by the pure guesswork of later glorifiers. By a true discoverer, we mean one who not only finds unknown land, but tells, writes, or sends back word about his discovery.

In another way than by helping to populate its shores, the Japanese contributed very efficiently to the historic discovery of America, in 1492. We are learning more and more to look into *all* the causes of a great event or movement, such as the revelation of a new world. We know that a good deal more than the dream of Columbus, or the favor or disfavor of a Spanish king and queen, was behind the discovery of this continent.

One must know the history of the world in order to understand that of the United States. The coast-line of Africa was first explored and the new water route eastward to India found by the Portuguese. Then came the thought of sailing westward to get to India on the other side. All the first discoverers of America were Italians, — Columbus, the Cabots, Vespucci, Verrazano, and Fray Marcus. Why and how did Portugal lead the world in discovery? And why did Italy follow so soon after?

It was because the eastern routes by sea and land, over the Mediterranean and by caravans, were shut up, completely stopping all trade.

Who shut them? We answer, first the Saracens in North Africa, and then the Turks in Constantinople.

Yet, what moved the Turks westward from their old ancestral seats around the Caspian Sea, causing them to advance to the west upon Syria, Constantinople, and the old Byzantine Empire, and into Egypt? The Saracens had, centuries before, overflowed North Africa and even occupied much of

E

Spain and Portugal, but the Turks completely blocked the only remaining routes north and south to the Indies. What led or drove the Turks into their western movement, making them press upon Europe?

To this we answer, It was the Mongols, and the Mongols were very probably led by a Japanese.

The story is a very simple one. By the twelfth century, after several hundred years of fighting, all the tribes and peoples in the Japanese Islands had been conquered and brought under the sway of that conquering tribe from the Asian Highlands, which had discovered, explored, and colonized Japan, and pacified its savages or " Indians." The head of this tribe was the Mikado (a title meaning Holy Gate or Sublime Porte), a religious as well as a political chief, who, at Kioto, combined Church and State in his person just as the Sultan does in Constantinople. After the wars of exploration and conquest had ceased and peace had come, the two great, noble families, the Héiki and the Genji, or the Whites and the Reds, quarrelled. Then they broke into a feud which later kindled the flames of strife throughout the whole empire. It was like the civil War of the Roses in England. At first, the Héiki were successful and killed or banished the Genji leaders.

In 1159 Tokiwa, the beautiful concubine of the Genji leader, fled with her three children, not knowing where her future food and shelter were to be. One of her children was a babe at the breast. Captured by her lord's enemy, she saved her own life and that of her children by entering the harem of her conqueror. To make a long and fascinating story short, one of her sons grew up to be the mighty leader, Yoritomo. Another, the babe, became Yoshitsuné, the field-marshal, who annihilated the Héiki, after several campaigns, from 1180–85, finishing with a great naval battle at Shimonoséki (where the treaty between Japan and China was signed in May, 1895). This son of Tokiwa was the most brilliant of all Japan's mediæval generals.

When the people declared that the glory of the victories was due to Yoshitsuné, his older brother, Yoritomo the Tycoon, now that he had exhausted the benefit of his younger brother's service, became bitterly jealous of him. The spark was fanned to flames by a slanderer. The older persecuted his younger brother and finally ordered his death. Yoshitsuné fled northward to the island of Yezo and thence escaped to Tartary. In Chinese pronunciation his name was Genghi Khé. There are good arguments for thinking that it was this Japanese field-marshal who organized the Mongol tribes into that mighty host, which poured victorious out of their northern highlands upon the warm, rich lands of China. The Mongols conquered the great Chinese world, which included the Middle Kingdom and many vassal nations. Then this great cavalry leader, now known as Genghis Khan, whose genius both for war and peace resembled that of Napoleon, swept westward with his irresistible horsemen. He died in 1227; but under his successors the Mongol empire spread westward until it touched the Caspian Sea.

In the succeeding generations, the son and grandsons of Genghis continued his work of conquest, and their realm covered almost all Asia from Korea to Syria, as well as large portions of Russia. This invasion of the Mongols, even greater than those of their ancestors from the steppes, the Scythians and Huns, caused the establishment of many dynasties famous in history. It stirred up all Asiatic humanity to a movement westward, even as the missionary wars of Mahomet had forced them northward and the North Africans westward. The Turkomans and the various tribes of Turks were pushed and excited to action by the Mongols. Later, one branch of the great clan penetrated India, and is known in history as the line of the Mogul emperors whose splendid empire began in the fifteenth century.

Almost all the rulers of nations in Asia, except in Arabia and the purely Turkish dominions, became vassals of Khublai Khan, the grandson of

Genghis Khan. The Mongols even entered Europe, occupying for several generations large parts of Russia. These men from China, aided by the Arabs, brought with them not only the Chinese myths and notions of alchemy, magic, and fancy, but also Chinese arts and inventions, the magnetic needle, wall-paper, gunpowder, and printing, which spread westward. The old-world myths and fairy tales had almost as much influence on the romance and fact of the discovery and exploration of America as did the realities of compasses, globes, and maps, as we shall see. The mariner's compass — long known in China, and whose use in a voyage from Nankin to Korea in A.D. 1122 is recorded — came into Italy by the sea-route.

While the Mongols were in power, laws were modified, literature and public works flourished, and order was maintained over all Asia. Good roads were kept open and a general spirit of toleration prevailed. The Nestorian Christians entered the Chinese empire in welcome. They converted the royal family of a Tartar tribe, living near Lake Baikal in Mongolia, where now Russian steamers ply and the Siberian railway passes. Noticing the similarity in sound of the Tartar chief's title, "Owang Khan," to the Hebrew Cohen or Kahna, priest, and Johann, John, the Europeans called him Prester John, that is, Priest John. This famous

character, who in 1202 became the vassal of Genghis
Khan, issued letters to the Pope and Kings of France
and Portugal. He long survived, in western poetry
and legend, as the priestly ruler of an earthly para-
dise. The legend of Prester John powerfully influenced the Spanish friars in America, who hoped
to find some such prince and convert him to the
church.

CHAPTER VI.

WHILE the Franks, or the peoples in Europe which afterwards became nations, — Italian, German, French, Spanish, — were developing their history during the middle ages, Arabia was considered the land of spices. This was not because these aromatic plants grew there, but because in the Arabian ports were the markets to which the spices of India and the Malay archipelago were brought. The Arabs, as we know from their own geographers, traded in the far East not only with China, but even with Korea. In Spain, with their universities, learned men, books, libraries, and science, the Saracens taught much to the Christian nations, then only partially risen out of their semibarbarism. In time, Moorish Spain became the centre of science in Europe.

From the ninth to the fifteenth century the Europeans knew little about the world, except what the learned men could gather from the ancient authors, Strabo and Ptolemy. Much of their

knowledge of countries, and even their idea of the
roundness of the earth, was obtained from the old
Greeks through Arabic translations. During the
Renaissance, or rebirth of knowledge, art, and literature in the fifteenth century, the ancient Latin
and Greek authors were eagerly read. This discovery of the ancient world of books, statues, coins, and
ideas was almost as wonderful as the finding out of
a new continent. As Moorish Spain had led in
science, so Italy was pioneer in literature and phi-
losophy, thus powerfully influencing all the nations
in this awakening of curiosity to know about the
world. Of the Italian cities, Pisa and Florence
became centres of art and science, while Venice
and Genoa excelled in Oriental commerce.

For over half a century there was much commerce between Venice and Genoa and the Mogul
and Chinese empires, or India and Cathay. The
Italian merchants used to bring from Asia, silks,
cashmeres, muslins, dyewood, perfumes, spices, gold,
precious stones, and pearls. They used to boast
that no one in Europe could spice wine or season
meat without helping to enrich one of these Italian
cities. Their fleets traded directly with every maritime country in Europe, as well as with the near
and the far East.

A great many arts and sciences have arisen out
of the need of men to fill their stomachs and please

their appetites. In our day, we raise a variety of fruits and garden vegetables at home, and import eatables of all sorts from many countries, which our ancestors did not have; but we, too, enjoy spices for the flavor they give. Formerly, spices grew only in the far East. Now they are produced in all hot countries, and we have introduced many of the Oriental fruits and plants in our gardens. Until within a century or two, however, most people in Europe had to live chiefly on salt or fresh meat and fish and grain, with little in the way of salads or esculents, and in winter, their diet was especially restricted. So they enjoyed all the more the flavors of the aromatic nuts, seeds, rinds, barks, roots, and dried fruits used in cookery, or ground fine to sift on choice dishes. At dinner, a seat near the spice-box was the seat of honor. The very word "spice," from "specie," means kind; that is, *the* kind of delicacy, just as "specie" means, not paper, but the right kind of, money. Cloves, ginger, allspice, nutmeg, cardamon, pepper, mace, capsicum, cinnamon, cassia, and vanilla were all in demand. Many others, with names too hard to pronounce, were also imported at high prices. Of not a few of these spicy or piquant barks, herbs, or nuts thus imported at great expense, it was believed that they would heal man's aches, pains, and diseases, or keep them off. It was for the Oriental spices, even more than for silk and gold, that the southern Europeans were so eager to trade with the infidels further south and east.

The Genoese usually took the northern route by way of Constantinople and the Black Sea. They loaded their ships with goods brought either from the Caspian Sea region and China by caravan, or from India through the valley of the Euphrates, the Tigris, and the Persian Gulf. The traffic was partly by camels overland, and partly by river boats and sea-going ships. Thus India, China, and the Malay archipelago, full of spice islands, poured their wealth into sunny Italy, which grew rich and cultured, and finally became the bestower of light, science, wealth, and comfort upon all Europe, besides being the mother of the discoverers of America.

At this time Italy was divided into many powerful municipal republics, — Venice, Genoa, Pisa, Florence. The Venetians had not only a great rich city built upon piles in the lagoons of the Adriatic Sea, but also many neighboring and subject lands which ministered to their glory, fame, and wealth. The symbol of Venice was the lion of St. Mark, who was her patron saint. Her ships sent after Arabian goods took the southern route and sailed to the eastern end of the Mediterranean, where caravans from Cairo met them. By this means, the Venetians had a longer water route than the Genoese, but one that required constant skill to navigate, and not a little military force and fighting to keep open. In time, it got to be quite common for Italian travellers and merchants to visit Arabia and go to Mecca. Besides her trade, Venice had famous manufactories. Here were made most of the beads and many of the glass and metal trinkets used later in the traffic with the Africans and Americans. One gentleman, now living in the Mohawk valley, has duplicated in Venice shops or museums every pattern of the beads, which he found by the hundreds, in the Iroquois Indian graves in New York.

The Venetians and the Mongols got along very well together. Princes, envoys, and merchants from Europe visited the court of the Great Khan, and Italian artists and decorators in India helped to build and beautify the mosques and minarets and tombs of Mogul India; perhaps even the Taj Mahal.

Among other travellers in the far East, who heard also of Japan, were Matteo and Nicolo Polo, who made two overland journeys from Italy to China. On their second journey, in 1271, they carried letters from Pope Gregory X. to the Chinese Emperor, who was then a Mongol, and called the Great Cham, or Khan. With them

went Marco Polo, who spent many years as an
officer in the service of the Khan, visiting Tibet,
Persia, and southern China.   For three years he
was governor of a large city.   These Venetians in
the Chinese empire used the paper money and
passports then in common use, and saw the Grand
Canal, which, though dug long before, had been
greatly improved by the Khan.   They heard stories
of Japan and of its gilded roofs, gold-plated pagodas
and temples, of which the columns and water-gutters
under the eaves were of gold.

Centuries afterward, when living in Japan, I my-
self saw castle towers tipped with golden-scaled
bronze dolphins which flashed high in the air, and
temple roofs with heavy and wide eaves-troughs
made of solid gold, which were set to catch the
sacred droppings of the rain from heaven.   I saw
also virgin gold coins as big as a man's extended
hand, besides temple pillars and ceilings and forests of idols covered with gold-leaf.

When the mighty Mongol Armada was in preparation to sail on its vain attempt to conquer
Japan, the Polos taught the Mongols how to make
catapults and other European engines of war.

These Venetians were in Cathay, or the Chinese
empire, over twenty years.   They then returned by
way of Persia, arriving in Italy in 1295.   When
Marco Polo wrote his wonderful book, telling of

the marvellous curiosities of China, and about the
brave Japanese who fought the Mongol Armada,
and cut off the heads of the great Khan's messengers, he was laughed at. He spelled and pronounced the Chinese name, Shi-pen-kok (meaning
Sun-root Land, or Kingdom of the Rising Sun)
as Cipango or Zipangu, and China (Katai) as
Cathay. His book was at first branded as a mass
of falsehoods, and in derision he was called "Signor
Milliano," or "Lord Millions," because he used the
word "million" so often. Gradually, his story was
found to be true.

There is little doubt but that Columbus read
Polo's book a great deal, and thought much about
what he had said concerning Cathay, or China, and
Zipangu, or Japan. Franciscan friars also visited
China, and Christian churches were begun in several Chinese cities. Embassies from the Pope and
the Khan exchanged courtesies at Avignon and
Peking. Cathay and Cambaluc (China and Peking)
became well known in Europe. Italian merchants,
doctors, and priests travelled and lived in Chinese
cities; and, on the other hand, Chinese engineers
and physicians won fame in Persia.

From the thirteenth to the fifteenth century was
the golden age of Italian commerce with the East,
when gems, rich silks, gold and silver, jewelled
arms and armor, statues, pictures, and palaces were

more plentiful in Italy than anywhere else in
Europe. The Venice of our century is only a
shadow of its former greatness. As long as the
Eastern trade continued, Columbus was not likely
to go to the poor West, or to Spain; nor was any
new world toward the sunset likely to be discovered.

But suddenly (as it seems in history, though in
reality, gradually) the trade routes were blocked,
commerce ceased, and Italy became poor. Why?
we ask, and the answer is, Because of tremendous
political changes in Asia, but chiefly on account of
Mahometan bigotry.

In Asia, with the one exception of Japan (which
has the longest continuous line of rulers in the
world), dynasties do not last long, and political
structures are not permanent. The great Mongol
empire, after scarcely more than a century of life,
was broken into fragments. In 1368, the Chinese
rebelled against their Mongol rulers and set up
the Mings, a native line of emperors; but Confu-
cianism became more narrow and severe. Many
of the nations once under the great Mongol
Khan were converted from gentle and tolerant
Buddhism to intolerant Islam, which teaches that
men of other faiths should be put to the
sword.

The empire of Timour rose in Central Asia, and

between the years 1360 and 1405 Timour conquered most of western Asia, including Syria and
Asia Minor, invaded Russia to Moscow, defeated
the Turks in battle, and forced other nations to
acknowledge his power. But when Timour died of
ague in 1405, the Turks were left free to press their
conquest of the Greek Christian empire, and to advance on Constantinople.

The Saracens had long held Spain and Portugal,
Egypt and North Africa; but while Christian valor
was driving the Mahometans out of Europe, other
influences were at work to usher in a new era of
knowledge about the earth on which men lived, and
which some thinkers suspected was a round planet.
In this century, also, wood-engraving, printing,
paper, the rousing of energies by the fierceness of
the Turks, and the cutting off of old luxuries and
supplies, stirred and widened the thoughts of men,
compelled new enterprises, and paved the way for
the discovery of America. The introduction and
improvement of the mariner's compass, and the
invention of the astrolabe, or star-catcher, for taking the position of the heavenly bodies, greatly
aided navigation.

One of the first countries to explore the sea for
new trade routes, to attempt to reopen traffic with
the Orient, to set out in quest of new lands, and, if
possible, of Christian friends, to begin the mighty

work of uniting the nations of the earth, and to
make the explorations and settlements which the
Dutch first, and the English afterwards, confiscated
and appropriated, was little Portugal.   To this
country let us now look.

CHAPTER VII.

DOWN in the southwest corner of Europe is a
country now very much impoverished, often
made miserable by earthquakes, and kept poor by
superstition and the ignorance of its people. It
forms part of that Iberian peninsula which is shut
off by mountains and the sea from the rest of
Europe. Having plenty of rivers, the country is
like a great vineyard, for here is the climate in
which grapes grow luxuriantly. Instead of the
northern butter and beer, there is plenty of oil and
wine. Oporto gives its name both to its rich and
heavy port wine, and to the kingdom itself. In
ancient times this city was named Cale, and the
Latin words " Portus Cale," meaning the port or
gate to Cale, have become Portugal. Anciently the
country was called Lusitania.

Although to-day poor, unrenowned, and one of
the lowest among the Powers of Europe, Portugal
was once a great nation. Here were first kindled
the bright beacon lights of modern discovery. In

the fifteenth century, the people of this kingdom led
in the making of modern geography. Best of all,
Portugal was pioneer in the growing federation of
nations which already exists under international
law, and which is yet to culminate in that unity of
the world which is implied in Christianity.

One feature that greatly influenced the maritime
and colonial polity of Portugal, was the peculiar
sentiment and national tone produced by its long
warfare against Mahometanism. In A.D. 711, Tarik
landed on the coast, and the Saracen occupied parts
of the Iberian peninsula for five or six hundred
years. The splendid Moorish cities, palaces, and
gateways, still remaining in Spain, date from this
era. When the Christians began to lift their heads
and drive back the Saracens, Portugal was one of
the first Christian kingdoms formed. This fight for
life continued during several hundred years. It was
one of religion, of race, and of civilization for the
Fatherland. The Moors fought the duel bravely,
and were only driven away, inch by inch, from the
soil of the Iberian peninsula. We ought to excuse,
or at least be ready to explain, much of the peculiar
religious bigotry of the Spaniards and Portuguese of
early days, because of their long struggle for life and
faith against equally bigoted Mahometans.

It was because Prince Henry, born in 1394,
nearly a century before Columbus' discovery, and

called The Navigator, sought to continue this warfare of the cross against the crescent in every part
of the world, that Portugal became the first naval
academy in Europe, and trained up a line of discoverers. Prince Henry established, in 1415, a
school of navigation, in which noblemen were educated, and the sailor's craft made honorable. He
introduced the use of the astrolabe and the magnetic needle, or the mariner's compass. Set on
gimbals in a box, with a card or face marked with
thirty-two points, it was much improved over the
Chinese original. From this school, issued that
movement of maritime discovery and enterprise
which placed Portugal in the van of European
civilization. The coast-line of Africa was gradually learned, the route to the Indies reopened,
and Columbus stimulated to his discovery.

On the 4th of March, 1894, all Portugal was
ablaze with bunting and vocal with music, for the
people were everywhere celebrating the five hundredth anniversary of the sailor prince who never left
land, but who became the father of modern navigation. His captains discovered Africa, and he inspired Columbus. Through his influence, within
a century one-half of the globe was discovered.

Who was this Prince Henry, and how came his
call from God to open the East and West?

Henry was the son of King John (under whom

Portugal first began to drive back the Moors) and of Philippa, daughter of "old John of Gaunt, time-honored Lancaster." Trained to war, he, like so many soldiers of that age, might have spent his life in fighting for this king or that, in any cause that paid him well. In 1415 he went with his two brothers on an expedition against the Moorish rock-fortress and city of Ceuta in Morocco. So hard was the fighting and so gallant the bravery of the three princes, but especially of Henry, that in one day the place fell into the hands of the Christians.

So splendid became the fame of Prince Henry that, all at once, the Pope, the Emperor, and the Kings of Castile and of England invited the youthful hero to take command of their armies. But, instead of more glory and war, Prince Henry suddenly became a student, and faced for twelve long years costly failure and disheartening ridicule; yet he ever kept on dreaming of new countries and finding new paths in the sea. This seemed a conversion almost as wonderful as that of St. Paul. What, or who caused it?

Let us look at Ceuta. The name is probably a corruption of the Roman Septas, or seven. It is a twin rock opposite Gibraltar, and was one of the Pillars of Hercules, marking the end of the earth at which the whole ancient world had written, "ne

plus ultra "— no more beyond. It was Prince Henry
who rubbed out that legend, and bade men seek
further.

To-day, in America, — sometimes called by en-
vious Europeans, " the land of the almighty dollar,"—
those Pillars of Hercules survive in the sign for our
unit of value. In the graphic device " $\underline{S}$," we have
a skeleton picture of the two Pillars of Hercules,
of which Ceuta was one, with the tower flags or
streamers in between, in the form of a letter S.
The American silver dollar has replaced the old
Spanish " pillar dollar," or " piece of eight," but the
ghost of it remains in our writing. Whenever we
use commercial arithmetic, we borrow the Arabic
numerals brought by the Saracens, first from India
and then from Arabia, into Spain, and for our dollar
mark, we make a diagram of the two Pillars of Hercules, the twin rocks of Gibraltar and Ceuta with
the Christian flag of Spain flying where once the
crescent banner waved.

Ancient ideas shut up the world at Ceuta and
Gibraltar, as the Philistines shut up Samson. Prince
Henry, like the Hebrew giant, rose up out of sleep,
and carrying the bars and gates away with him,
opened that world, of which European people, from
the Pope to the peasant, were then ignorant.

Prince Henry found that some of his Moorish
prisoners in Ceuta, instead of being horned devils,

were polished gentlemen of noble rank, liberally educated and well travelled.   He treated them kindly.
They in return told of the great continent of Africa
where they lived; of the mountains, deserts, and
oases; of the city of Timbuctoo, with its ivory pal-
ace and gilded roofs; of the Niger River, of Guinea,
of Mozambique and Zanzibar.   Still further, they
thrilled the young Christian prince, their captor,
with stories of voyages to India, whence shiploads
of pearls and rubies, gold and spices, came to enrich
the Mahometans; of the huge animals; of amazing
forests and fruits, and of the populous countries of
the great continent over which blazed the Southern
Cross amid starry skies.

All this set Prince Henry's imagination on fire.
" Africa for Christ " became his watchword — to be
understood, of course, in his own way.   He used
his opportunity at once.   He was grandmaster of
the order of Christ, and had control of its vast revenues.   He was governor for life of Algarve, the
extreme southeastern province of Portugal and of
Europe.   At Sagres, down at the very tip of the
kingdom and the continent, he founded an observa-
tory, the first in Portugal.   He devoted himself to
the study of astronomy and mathematics.   He sum-
moned to his aid all the men skilled in navigation,
or in making maps or instruments, of whom he
could hear.   He trained up young Portuguese naval

officers, who became fearless captains. In a decade, he had won away from Venice and Genoa the monopoly of seamanship and natural science.

Henry was not always successful at first, and the nobles ridiculed him, complained of him for wasting money, as they said; but he persevered. Soon his ships began to creep out along the African coast. The Azores, the Madeiras, the Canaries, and the Cape Verde Islands were first discovered, and then colonized; so that, by A.D. 1420, they had become part of the kingdom. The song of the pretty yellow canary birds was heard on the continent. The island groups became vineyards. In 1434, Cape Bojador was reached. In 1443, Gonsalvez came back with a bag of gold-dust and ten black men. This was the beginning of the slave-trade to Europe. These Africans were sent to be seen by the Pope, who at once gave Prince Henry a title deed of the country from Cape Bojador to the Indies, that is of all Africa. From this time, a little black boy is seen attending as page, or leading the horse of nearly every prince in Europe.

Gradually the Portuguese captains became bolder. They drove their little ships down past Sierra Leone and along the grain, the gold, and the ivory coasts. Moving hundreds of miles toward the rising sun, yet ever keeping within sight of land, in 1440 they discovered Guinea. By 1446, fifty-one ships had visited Senegal. When the Turks were rushing into Constantinople, in 1453, the famous annalist, Azurara, wrote his chronicles of the discovery and conquest of Guinea. As he says in this wonderful book, "The Lord Prince (Henry) had five reasons for the discovery of foreign countries.

"First, to ascertain the truth about these regions, as it appeared to him that if he or some other lord did not attempt the discovery, no mariner or merchant would try the venture, as it is quite clear that such persons will navigate to places only where they can reap evident profits.

"Second, he thought that perchance some Christian country might be found, with which his friendship and commerce might be established.

"The third reason was that he wanted to know the true extension of Mussulman's power, his born and sworn enemy.

"The fourth reason was that during the thirty-one years that he had waged war against the Mussulmans, he had never found a single Christian prince that would help him for the love of Jesus Christ, and he might find in the undiscovered world some Christian power that would be his ally.

"Fifth, the great desire of augmenting and increasing the faith in our true religion."

With such motives, the highest that can animate man, and with others also, — making a mixture as

in most men and nations, — Portugal nobly started
on the career of exploration. Her ships kept ever
moving to the southward along the edge of the
dark continent. When Henry died, in 1460, eighteen hundred miles of new coast had been discovered
and explored; Portugal was not only the centre of
geographical interest and science, but also a magnet
drawing to itself the Italian mariners, map-makers
and scholars; and the good work, begun by Henry,
kept on.

The Guinea trade made Lisbon rich, and hither
flocked the Italian merchants, geographers, and
map-makers, whose occupation at home was gone,
and who did not care about the petty wars then going on in Italy. Here they talked about the roundness of the earth, and the belief that it was a globe
gained new adherents. Before 1470, Bartholomew,
the brother of Christopher Columbus, established
himself at the Portuguese capital to make maps of
the new discoveries in Africa; and there, sometime
before 1473, Christopher Columbus joined him. In
1477, Christopher made a voyage to Iceland, where
he heard of the westward sea-travels of Leif Erikson.

When Captain Diaz started on a voyage to reach
the very southernmost end of Africa, Bartholomew
Columbus joined him. They passed the mouth of
the Congo River, — that gateway into a great divis-

ion of Africa; and, in our day, associated with the names of Livingstone and Stanley, one of whom explored its cradle lands, and the other its course to the sea.

It was, in 1486, after fifty years of Portuguese enterprise, that Bartholomew Columbus, leaving his map-making, accompanied Captain Bartholomew Diaz, with whom, over five thousand miles from home, he reached the southern tip of Africa, which Diaz named the Cape of Storms. When they returned, the wise king, delighted with this logical result of Prince Henry's enlightened foresight, scratched out of the record in the log-book, "Cape of Storms," and wrote in its place a name which proved a prophecy, — "Cape of Good Hope"; for, with the eyes of faith, he already saw the all-sea route opened to the Indies. Prince Henry was vindicated. The next Portuguese fleet, with African pilots, sailed straight to India.

When Bartholomew Columbus told his brother what he had seen, Christopher was, more than ever, satisfied that the earth was round, and that by sailing west he could reach Japan, which, he thought, projected far out toward Europe. Meanwhile, the future world-giver kept on trying to persuade the King of Spain; but in order to "have two strings to his bow," he sent his brother Bartholomew to England to interest King Henry VII. in the idea of getting to Japan by the back door. Henry was slow in making up his mind, and by the time Bartholomew reached France, he heard of his brother Christopher's return homeward.

We must not forget that all this was before Columbus discovered some islands and parts of a continent that he never knew belonged to a new world. It was Prince Henry's and King John's naval and colonizing policy that prepared the way for the success of Columbus. It was because Portugal discovered the old world first, that the Genoese thought of, and was encouraged to find, the new one. On the German Behaim's globe, made in 1487, the Portuguese flag is marked on so many coasts, countries, and islands that it seems as if the only European country then likely to possess the earth was little Portugal. Even Siam and the Golden Chersonese, or Malay peninsula, are so marked. Japan looms largely, but no continent appears between Europe and Asia.

The King of Portugal kept on encouraging his brave navigators. When he died, his successor, Manoel, fitted out an expedition under Vasco da Gama, a gentleman in the king's household, who in 1497 reached India by an all-sea passage, and then bravely continued in his little ship the circumnavigation of the globe.

This first furrow round the world ploughed by

a ship's keel was followed by another made by the
Portuguese Cabral, who in 1500 started out with
eighteen ships, expecting to reach Farther India
where the spices grew, by following the route
opened by da Gama. Obeying his instructions, he
kept far out in the Atlantic, and, being driven still
further by storms, came in sight of Brazil by acci-
dent. He explored the coast, and took possession
of it. He then visited East Africa, Calcutta, and
Cochin China, reaching Lisbon July 23, 1501, with
an amazingly rich cargo of spices, which in those
days were often worth their weight in gold.

Vasco da Gama's second voyage was made with
twenty ships, in 1502–3; but no one circumnavigated the globe again until 1519, when the feat
was repeated by Magellan, a Portuguese, who had
been in the East Indies. Like so many others, he
considered America a barrier to the far East; but
knowing that Balboa had found an ocean behind it,
Magellan hoped to sail around the obstruction, and
thus get to the lands of spice, gold, silk, and gems.

Yet this squadron left Europe under Spanish
auspices, Magellan having quarrelled with the Portuguese Court, which he thought had treated him
meanly. Crossing the Atlantic, he passed through
the strait, which he named after himself. It was
a long while, however, before this watercourse
was used as a practical highway. Nevertheless,

Magellan's voyage and discovery gave to the world its first distinct knowledge of the Pacific. Soon afterwards, the Spanish discovery of the Philippines led to their colonization and the development of a rich commerce through Mexico to the Asiatic islands.

Even North American waters mirrored the flag of Lusitania. In 1500 Gaspar Cortereal ploughed the Atlantic, reaching the high latitudes of America, and finding amazing sea-wealth. Kidnapping some of the people, probably red Indians, he brought them home, and told also of the new-found fisheries. King Emanuel thought more of the promising resources of labor that would require no wages than of the fisheries. So he named this new slave-coast Terra de Labrador, or Land of Laborers, which name it still keeps.

No one can omit Portugal from the romance of discovery, or when telling the story of the finding of America, and of its size and shape. From far Formosa which the Portuguese named, and from Japan which a Portuguese, Mendez Pinto, was the first to enter and describe from sight, to Labrador, Portugal has a noble record of discovery.

If, at times, we are tempted to look with contempt upon little Portugal, because of her smallness and weakness, and to despise the country because of prevalent bigotry and ignorance, and her ap-

proval of the slave-trade in Africa, we must not
forget her history.   It is a great fact that the
Portuguese discovered the African continent, and
opened Asia; and this they did without undue vio-
lence.   Portugal, with the grandest of all motives
that can move mankind to action, — the motive of
religion, — bore the almighty spirit of civilization
round this orb to awaken slumbering races and
resuscitate dead nations.   It was Portugal that
brought separate communities together, and began
the assimilation of mankind to mankind.

CHAPTER VIII.

ITALY, by its shape and situation in the middle of southern Europe, very close to Africa, and not far from Asia, — a peninsula with many harbors, — was fitted from the first to be a land of ships and sailors, and the home of conquerors. Shaped like a boot, with a strong leg and unwearied foot inside of it, Italy seems to walk upon the sea.

Japan boasts herself as "the country within the four seas," but Italy and her islands are washed by five seas, — the Ligurian, the Tyrrene, the African, the Ionian, and the Adriatic, — all of them famous for their deep azure color, and for the phosphorescence of the water. Here grew up the Roman nation which, at first regal, then republican, and finally imperial, ran a splendid career of twelve hundred years. With its standing army of three hundred and fifty thousand men in fifty legions, and with a wonderful system of roads and laws, the Romans ruled the earth, from the Pillars of Hercules to the Cataracts of the Nile and from the Rhine River to the desert of Africa. The common idea of the

79

"world" to a Roman lay in the word "oikumené,"—
the inhabited part of the earth.

In the fifth century the Roman empire fell. For
five hundred years afterwards Italy was harassed by
the Barbarians who poured in from the North.
About the tenth century, the people of the towns
made struggles to govern themselves; and so there
grew up many city republics which built walls and
made themselves independent of the feudal lords or
nobles. In this way the famous cities of Pisa,
Florence, Venice, and Genoa sprang up.

At the head of the Adriatic, where seven or eight
rivers rolled down their mud and slime into the sea,
making many islands amid very shallow water, there
gradually collected together many rich people who
had fled from the interior cities, when the Huns,
under Attila, invaded Italy. There, forgotten by
the Roman rulers, and beyond the reach of the
Barbarians who had no ships, a population grew
up, supporting themselves by catching fish and
making salt. Each little island was a republic by
itself, but sent delegates who met in council and
elected a doge or duke. In A.D. 809 they made
choice of the island of Rialto, and built the city of
Venice as the capital of their republic.

Twenty years later they sent to Alexandria for
the body of St. Mark, and made him the patron of
their state. For centuries the lion of St. Mark

figured on all their arms, their banners, and their ships; and the cry, "Viva San Marco," inspired their courage in many a sea-fight. Millions of boys were named after the lion-like evangelist. For six centuries the Venetians maintained their independence against the Lombards on one side and the Saracens on the other. They greatly assisted the first crusaders with their fleets. They steadily enriched themselves by commerce with Asia and Africa, and extended their sway and influence over many subject and neighbor lands.

On the other side of Italy, a little further south, seated grandly on the sea, is the city of Genoa. Its splendid harbor is sheltered by the Apennine Mountains, and is safely enclosed with moles and masonry, against which the sea-waves break in vain. It already had a history when Rome and Carthage were contesting in a death struggle for the supremacy of the Mediterranean. In the sixth century, with the disruption of the Roman empire, it fell into the hands of the Lombards. Like the other Italian coast cities, it suffered so much from the Saracens that, in self-defence, its navy was enlarged, and thus was laid the foundation of its sea-power. In the eleventh century, when the western world warred with the Moslems for the sepulchre of Jesus, Genoa was a tremendous rival of Venice in the crusading business. Both were more eager for

G

the profit of transporting crusaders than for getting
possession of an empty tomb.   These two cities,
with Pisa, had then more vessels on the Mediterranean than all the rest of Christendom.   The
Genoese encouraged the crusaders with enthusiasm, enjoying the fat contracts made for conveying
them to Syria.

Within Genoa the Superb grew up great trading
firms and princely merchants who built magnificent
palaces.   In 1240 this marine republic was able to
place Michael, the ruler of her choice, upon the
throne of the Byzantine empire, and to receive, in
addition to her already extensive eastern possessions, the suburbs of Constantinople and the great
fort of Smyrna.   With Corsica, Minorca, Marseilles,
and Nice already in the hands of the Genoese, they
were able to control, not only, much of the Mediterranean commerce but also the northern overland
route to India through the Black and Caspian seas.
Thus Genoa became amazingly rich, and her sailors
were to be found in many seas, always ready to
trade and navigate, and to fight or to quarrel with
the rival galleys and ships from Venice.

In these democratic Italian republics, there was
much turbulence but also much independence of
spirit, the people being bold, energetic, and industrious.   The wealth and power of the Genoese
excited the jealousy and cupidity of invaders,

who several times conquered them; but patriots
always rose up to deliver and throw off the yoke.
One of these was the famous Andrea Doria, after
whom was named our first American ship of war,
which carried the Declaration of Independence, in
1776, to the Dutch Island of St. Eustacius in the
West Indies, where on the 16th of November, from
the Dutch governor and fort, our colors — the thirteen red and white stripes — received the first foreign salute ever fired in honor of the American
flag.

Genoa was under the control of France, and it
was the time of the greatest quarrels between her
nobles and people when the feuds of the Guelphs
and Ghibellines about which Dante has sung, were
at their height, when in the Colon family there
were born three sons, — Bartholomew, Christopher,
and Diego. The name "Colon" is Genoese. The
form "Columbus" is Latin, and means a dove, just
as does that of "Jonah," the Hebrew voyager. Each
of these sons grew up to be interested in ships,
voyages, and geography.

It is interesting to walk about Genoa, in the
streets where the Columbus boys played, to visit
the wharves and shore, over which they looked
towards the deep blue waters out of which would
sail and into which came the gay ships that sought
and brought the wonders of far-off countries. One

can go there to-day, as I have done, and lodge in
great gloomy hotels which were once mighty palaces.
For a little money, one can sleep in the banqueting
room or audience chamber of a former prince.

As Christopher grew up, he had to help his
father — a wool comber by trade — to earn a living
for the family; but he also went to school and
learned a good deal about geography, and to write
easily in Latin. In 1460, Christopher, when only
fourteen, took to the sea, becoming a cabin boy
and doing some other service that lads were able
to perform in the galleys of that day. Perhaps it
seemed then to him as if he might one day become
a merchant prince with many vessels; but an event
occurred, which disappointed hundreds of Genoese,
stopped their trade, ruined their merchant princes,
and turned the face of young Christopher from the
East to the West.

News came that the Turks had captured Constantinople, and soon the crest-fallen Genoese captains came sailing back with many empty ships.
They said that the Turks had refused to let them
pass into the Black Sea, except upon payment of
tolls so enormous that all profits would be lost.
Thus, at a blow, the rich trade with the East was
cut off, and Genoa, for a while, was miserably poor.
Perhaps the boy of seventeen did not care so much
about being an Indian merchant, for he kept on

studying geography and mathematics, and began to ask himself whether some other way could not be opened to the golden lands of Asia. He was not a young man to give up easily.

Probably about this time Columbus began to believe that the earth was round. Nearly two thousand years before, some unknown Greek had got hold of the idea, and the philosopher Aristotle and the geographer Strabo, had talked it over. Averroes, a Moorish scholar of the twelfth century, at Cordova in Spain, made the idea known in Europe. Albertus Magnus and Roger Bacon had also read of, and revived, the dream of a ball-like earth hanging in the air. When Alliacus made the idea popular in his book, " Imago Mundi," Columbus thought he would some day be able to prove it to all. In his various voyages and talks with sea-faring men he got many hints favoring the theory, and he noticed that ships would rise upon the horizon when coming toward him, and sink when going away. If the earth were round, why could he not find China by sailing the other way towards the west? He knew that Genoa, his native city, could not help him in his enterprises, though he earnestly entreated her to do so. Had Genoa been willing or rich enough to fit out ships for her son, the new world might have become the possession of this city republic.

It was in the year 1470, when either thirty-four
or twenty-four years old, that his brother Bartholomew went to Lisbon, as we have seen, and set up
in business as a map-maker, selling his goods to the
many sea-captains at that port.   Columbus followed
his brother, and also drew maps, and made voyages.
He became ardently interested in the successes of
Prince Henry's navigators, but he thought out
another way of steering.   In 1474, he began cor-
responding with the Italian geographer Toscanelli,
who assured him that his plan of a voyage was
practicable, and that he could reach Cathay by sailing westward three thousand miles.   He now began
to broach his proposition to the King of Portugal,
arguing that such a voyage would greatly enrich
his possessions and wealth.   Meanwhile, he married
a lady named Felipa Moniz, and probably had three
children.   One of these, Ferdinand, wrote the biog-
raphy of Columbus, which is the basis of almost all
the narratives written about the man who gave a
new world to Spain.

Enthusiastic as Columbus was, everything seemed
to confirm his ideas.   In 1477 he made a voyage to
the far North, reaching Iceland, and learning about
Leif Erikson and Thorfinn's trips to Vineland.   He
was thus still further assured.   In those days, fighting, trading, slave-catching, and slave-selling were
often done by the same crew in the same vessel.

Columbus had experiences in a slave-trading expedition to Guinea, and went on piratical expeditions several times; but while his brother would sail east, Christopher insisted on sailing west.

Christopher got tired of trying to do anything in Portugal, and started off for Spain to interest the monarchs, Ferdinand and Isabella, leaving word to have his brother go to England and plead his western scheme with King Henry VII. While Columbus chafed and worried in Spain, cooling his heels in waiting upon the King and Queen, mocked by the boys who thought him a crank, getting poorer and poorer, bearing the ridicule of the Council, the gray hairs multiplying in his beard and hair, he learned of his brother's voyage to the Cape of Good Hope. This only made him the more resolved to sail the contrary way toward the setting sun.

Spain had then a good many reasons for not wanting to risk men, money, or ships in a project that seemed like trying to make water run up hill. In the first place, the central government was not yet strong, or perfectly certain of getting control of all the provinces or of driving out the Moors. The people were poor after the long wars. The plague was sweeping off thousands. The Inquisition was not yet a financial success. It had spent more money to carry on the hellish work than it got in revenue by confiscating the estates of Jews and Moors and other people called " heretics."

The government would not say either Yes or No to Columbus. The learned men to whom the matter was referred, — most of whom were too old to entertain a new idea, — were yet not unanimous, one way or the other ; and while the Court was moving about from camp to castle, a long and patient hearing of the whole case could not be given. Meanwhile, Columbus, though probably fifty-six years old and his beard getting grayer, kept on arguing. His new friends also firmly supported his views. When, finally, the last crescent flag had been lowered, and the silken banners of the cross waved high in air above the Moorish citadel of Granada, there was no further excuse to postpone the final decision.

Yet at this moment, Christopher, hopeless, hungry, and footsore, stood with his little son at the door of the monastery La Rábida, and begged for food. The abbot, who heard his story with patience, had been at one time confessor of the Queen, and now thought he might have some influence at Court. So he went to see the Queen who was, indeed, like her Syrian namesake, a Jezebel to heretics, but a lovely and Christian Queen to her friends. The good abbot was successful. A court suit was obtained for Columbus, who presented himself before

CHRISTOPHER COLUMBUS AT THE LA RABIDA MONASTERY.

the sovereigns at the city of the holy faith, Santa Fé,
— a name which has been duplicated in our territory of New Mexico.

At first, the whole project seemed to be wrecked
because Christopher's terms were too high. He
wanted to be made admiral of the ocean and viceroy
of all the lands he should discover; to keep possession of one-tenth of all the gold and other wealth that
might be acquired, and to have all his rights and
titles made hereditary. The King was unable at
first to agree to these demands, for while to Christopher the scheme was as reality, to Ferdinand it was
as a dream. So the Genoese came away once more
disheartened, but firm in his claim. Nevertheless
three good friends — one a court lady, and another a
royal minister, and the greatest, the Queen — caught
enthusiasm from the dreamer, and prevailed with
the King. Christopher was called back, and the
compact was signed April 17, 1492.

CHAPTER IX.

IT was not until Friday, August 3, 1492, that the three ships and crews were ready. As a punishment for some offence, the people of Palos were condemned to furnish three vessels with all proper equipments. It is more than probable that Jewish merchants assisted with money in the enterprise.

It was hard, however, to get a crew to start out under a man who was supposed to be nursing a crazy notion. Even by emptying the prisons and pardoning debtors and criminals, who were released on their promise to enlist as sailors, the necessary number of one hundred and twenty men was long in being made up; for, after the jail birds were free, many deserted. The quality of the men who were finally obtained did not increase the chances of success.

Christopher's motive was perfectly clear. In his journal of the voyage, he says, in the introduction, that he was sailing with one object in view, which was to reach the dominion of the great Mongol

Khan, — a line of sovereigns established most probably, as we have seen, by the Japanese Yoshitsuné. In fact, the Genoese was over a century behind the times, for the Mongol power in China had fallen a hundred and fifty years before, and the Ming dynasty of pure Chinese emperors had been reigning in Nanking since 1368. But there were no telegraphs or newspapers then, and the Turks had for many years shut off all tidings from the far East. As for Japan, which he hoped to reach, the end of the fifteenth century was the poorest and most miserable time in its history. The King of Spain, however, knew no more than the Genoese.

This is what Columbus wrote:

" In consequence of the information which I had given to your Highnesses of the lands of India and of a Prince, who was called the Grand Khan . . . therefore your Highnesses determined to send me, Christopher Columbus, to see the said Prince and the people and lands . . . and ordered that I should not go by land to the East, by which it is the custom to go, but by a voyage to the West, by which course, unto the present time, we do not know *for certain* that any one has passed."

The Italics are ours. It is probable that Columbus did not know *for certain*, that any one had sailed far westward into the Atlantic, though it is quite probable that he had heard of the discoveries of the Norsemen. He must surely have known of the voyages of the English sailors and others who made voyages far out into the Atlantic to find Antilia or the island of the Seven Cities, of which we shall hear more. On the chart of the globe which he had made himself, Japan stands out prominently between Europe and Africa, not, as it really is, long and narrow between Kamtchatka and the Philippines, but very broad from east to west, as if squeezed flat to fit the theory. Indeed, it was wonderfully like a modern railway map on which distances are lengthened or shortened to suit the advertisement. The whole region under attention is squeezed out of proportion, so as to gain patrons or furnish a quick view.

Christopher had the mariner's compass, derived from China, but greatly improved. He had also the astrolabe, introduced or at least made popular by Prince Henry, with which he could find out his position by taking observations of the stars or sun.

Best of all, he had profound faith — in God, in the possibility of success, and in his personal mission. He and his men went to church to ask the divine blessing upon their adventure. Then, although it was Friday, Admiral Columbus sailed away a half-hour before sunrise.

His little squadron consisted of the ship *Santa Maria*, or *Holy Mary*, of one hundred tons' burden;

with two caravels named *Nina* and *Pinta.* Only
the ship was decked, each of the other vessels having but a light floor at bow and stern.

- The caravels got their name from beetles, being the
same as the Egyptian " scarab," — the word "cara-
vel" meaning a little beetle. They were narrow at
the poop and wide at the bow. Each had four
masts and a bowsprit. The principal sails were
lateen ; that is, sails fastened at the top along the
boom, which was coupled at the centre of the mast,
while the lower ends of the sails were held by ropes
tied at the base of the ship. Extending from little
masts on the bow were two square sails. In those
days everything was rich in color, and the painted
canvas sails were magnificent with designs of the
cross, the heraldry of the King of Spain, the arms
of Aragon and Castile, and the images of the bleed-
ing Christ. Nevertheless, these caravels were very
disagreeable sea-craft with which to attempt a long
voyage.

Reaching the Canary Islands, the frontier of the
old world, several weeks were lost in mending
the clumsy rudder of one vessel, and in altering
the sail of another. At last, on September 6, they
began, as it seemed to the men, climbing up the
water-hill of the world and sliding down on the
other side, until the islands faded from sight. Then
there were weeping eyes. Bearded men broke out

into bitter lamentations, because they had bidden farewell to " the habitable world."

Hundreds of years afterwards, orators and essay-ists wishing to magnify Christopher Columbus and move their auditors by exciting in them enthu-siasm or religious jealousy, hatred, or prejudice, have tried to tell a wonderful story of mutiny, to show that the Admiral's life was in danger. They have striven to crowd into this journey on the water awful and significant adventures; but, as a matter of fact, it was a very ordinary, hum-drum voyage. The simple truth is, as we read it in his own diary of the cruise, only one thing seemed very wonderful to Columbus himself. That was the variation of the magnetic needle, which trem-bled away to the northwest rather than to the northeast. This phenomenon startled the Ad-miral, and especially his subaltern and crew.

When thirty-one days out from sight of land, a flock of birds — not sea-gulls or petrels — flew in front of the ship, moving to the southwest. Seeing them, Alonzo Pinzon, captain of the *Pinta*, begged Columbus to follow in their track. The Admiral yielded, and these land birds became pilots to the Spaniards.

Thus it came to pass that He who guides the raven and sees the sparrow fall, ordered that the Latin emigrants and civilization should find their home in central and southern America, while the northern and better America should be as yet unknown.

Still the ships kept on. On the evening of the thirty-fifth day, even while Admiral Christopher was wondering whether, after all, he should have to turn back to satisfy the clamors of his men, he saw ahead a light. Early in the morning of Thursday, October 11, a sailor in the top shouted the good news, — "Land!" Soon the sun rose, revealing the low, sandy shore of Watling's Island, around part of which they had sailed during the night.

With fine dress and banners, and all display of costume and weapons, appropriate for the significant ceremony, Admiral Columbus in a panoply of steel, and his men in armor, landed. According to the custom of discoverers, and in signification of possession, Columbus and his men kneeled and kissed the ground. With wet eyes, they poured out their thanksgiving to God. Then, with the ceremonies of the church, Columbus planted the banners of Aragon and Castile. The splendid colors waved to the wind, while he took possession of the country for Ferdinand and Isabella and their viceroy, Columbus.

The natives called the land "Cat Island," but Columbus baptized it "San Salvador," or "Holy Saviour." One of the first questions he asked was whether this was Japan, but the only answer, and, indeed, the only conversation possible, was by signs. Thinking that any land that was not of Europe must be of Asia, and that he was in the Indies, he called the people "Indians." One of the first things he noticed was that some of the men wore pieces of gold hung from their noses, and Columbus was anxious to know whether they had more. By signs they informed him that "there was a king in the south who owned many vessels filled with gold."

Perhaps these islanders had in mind the gilded chieftain in South America, who, when elected, powdered himself with gold, and then, going out on a gold-decorated raft to the middle of a lake, plunged in and washed off the gold-dust as an offering to the goddess of the lake. From this moment began a quest of the golden man and the chasing of phantoms that led thousands of Spaniards to miseries of hunger and thirst, starvation and death.

The Spaniards also visited other Bahama Islands, and then landed on Cuba in November. Pinzon was the discoverer of Hayti, or San Domingo, though he got no credit for it. The party spent most of the winter in the delightful climate, though losing the *Santa Maria* by shipwreck. However, the Admiral saved her timbers, and with them built a fort on the northern side of Hayti, to which he gave the name of " Little Spain," or " Hispaniola." As he had stepped upon this island on Christmas Day, he called the place " Nativity," or " Birth-day," " La Navidad." Everywhere the people were friendly, for the Spaniards seemed like visitors from heaven. The natives were soon cruelly un-deceived.

Columbus thought that it would be easy for his men to get along very well with such gentle people. So he selected forty men from his crew, which would be rather crowded on the two vessels remaining, and left them to form the first European settlement in the new land.

Then, after salutes and farewells, he turned his two prows homeward, and after a very stormy voyage, he arrived safely March 15, 1493. He and his companions were welcomed as those who had come back from the dead.

II

CHAPTER X.

THE westward movements of men from the sea
of Japan to the Bosphorus drove the Greek
scholars of Constantinople all over Europe, and the
Italian mariners to the maritime states facing the
Atlantic. Christopher Columbus became the most
famous of all, because, although he did not discover
the American continent, he was original and daring
in sailing westward across the Atlantic.

Columbus did not get many thanks or much honor,
after the first splendid reception awarded him by King
Ferdinand and Queen Isabella. Indeed, nobody
supposed that he had discovered a new world, but
only some projecting land or islands running out
from the Asian continent. Nevertheless, it was believed that he had found a new pathway to the Indies.
At once there began a great rivalry, with the possibilities of a bitter quarrel, between Portugal and
Spain, just as there had been between Venice and
Genoa, but with new features added. As Venice
had enjoyed the southern, and Genoa the northern
route to the riches of Asia, so Portugal, having

opened the southern path to India, feared that
Spain, by taking the northern or western route,
would gain even more wealth. The Portuguese regarded Columbus as being only a disciple of Prince
Henry, who had won success by following his
methods.

What promised to be a dangerous quarrel was
averted by an Italian prince, living in Rome, who
ruled a small territory called the States of the Church
around the city on the Tiber, in area about the size
of Maryland and Delaware. Italians were first to
discover and then to divide the world. This Italian
prince, the Pope, was then considered to be the
head of all the Christian churches, except the Greek
Catholic church, which extended over Russia and
Greece. At that time it was believed that the
whole world was under papal control, because the
Pope claimed to be the vicar of God. The nations
of the earth not yet known — it was thought —
ought to be, and sooner or later would be, under
the control of the spiritual head of the church.

During the middle ages, most men held the
same idea about the dominance of the religious over
the political organization of society, — of Church
over State, — as was common in such countries as
Russia, Turkey, China, Japan, and the African kingdoms. Such ideas have for the most part died out
of the world, or are steadily sinking out of sight, but

formerly they were very powerful. No king or
nation would have thought of owning any land
which the sailors or foreigners in their employ
had discovered, unless claim to ownership was first
ratified by the Pope.

In accordance with the ideas of the age, the Pope,
in decrees called bulls (from the "bulla" or round
seal), had already confirmed Portugal in the possession of the islands and countries of Africa discovered by its people. Knowing this, as soon as
Columbus had returned, Ferdinand applied to the
Italian Pope-Prince, as his spiritual superior, to
confirm the Spanish claims to the countries beyond
the western ocean already sighted or which might
be discovered. Pope Alexander VI. in his bull of
demarcation, dated May 3, 1493, confirmed the
Spanish claim. Drawing a line from north to
south out in the Atlantic Ocean, three hundred
miles west of the Azores, where the compass
pointed exactly north, his Holiness divided the
world in two portions. All lands newly discovered
by the Portuguese, which did not belong to any other
Christian prince on the east of this line were to be
the property of Portugal. Everything, not already
possessed by Christians west of the line, was to be
Spain's. Thus, as easily as a boy divides an apple,
the Pope cut the world in half.

This at first satisfied the Portuguese, but later they

petitioned their spiritual superior to draw the line
eight hundred miles farther west. His Holiness
assented, and a treaty between Spain and Portugal
was signed June 7, 1494. By this clever arrange-
ment, the Portuguese held possession of Brazil after
it had been discovered by Cabral in 1500, though
Pinzon the Spaniard had made landfall on its coast
earlier in the same year.

Thus it came to pass, that the Pope became one
more of those Italians who busied themselves with
the new world, its discoveries, and its conquests, and
yet who never owned a foot of land within it. Of
such Italians there were many, and Italy sent forth
the sowers to make harvest fields for others to reap.
" Unhappy Italy that beats the bush, while others
catch the bird," wrote Peter Martyr. Portugal
founded a school for navigators. Italy sent out
the pioneers. Spain won the new world and lost it.
France founded a vast, but transient empire. England did least exploring, yet founded a new nation.

It was not only the seafaring people of Venice
and Genoa who found their occupation gone when
the Turks blocked the eastern trade routes, but also
many others in Italian cities who directly or indirectly had been growing rich by the lucrative traffic
in spices and gold. It is in the latter half of the
fifteenth century that we find Italian merchants,
bankers, engineers, artists, and skilled mechanics

moving northward and settling in France and Germany, and in the Netherlands (or lowlands of western Europe, which are now Belgium and Holland), and in England.

In the large cities of these countries, one can see to-day more than one " Lombard Street," where the business men from Lombardy had their banking offices, goldsmiths' shops, and warehouses. Other thoroughfares and many families in Europe and America are named after Italian cities, places, and persons. The Longo-bards, or long-bearded barbarians, anciently from northwestern Germany, after centuries of residence in Italy, had become keen and shrewd money-lenders and merchants. At this time also, in England especially, but also in the Netherlands, Italian mechanics, engineers, and doctors found employment and introduced many good ideas and inventions. Italian was studied, and notably influenced the English language and literature. Fleets of Venetian and Genoese ships found that trade with Netherlands and England, though not, indeed, so profitable as with the East, was well worth cultivating and increasing. Antwerp became a very rich city, with its harbor ever full of ships, while London and Norwich, the two largest English business centres, also profited by this commerce. Their shops and stores were full of Italian novelties and the rich dresses, fashions, and notions

imported from the Mediterranean nations. The
jewels, stuffs, pictures, art works, rugs, and carpets
from Italy beautified English noblemen's castles,
the houses of the court ladies and gentlemen, and
rich merchants' dwellings.

At that time Bristol, in Devonshire, with its
curious little narrow, but deep, Avon stream, the
river of Wyckliffe and Shakespeare, was the chief
western seaport of the country, and had a good
trade with the southern countries. There was living here with his wife and three sons, a Venetian
merchant and navigator, whose name in its English
form is John Cabot. He had travelled in Arabia,
and had been at Mecca, where he saw many caravans, as in the days of Joseph and the Midianites,
laden with balm and spicery. On inquiry, he found
that they came from the far East. Like most educated Italians, Cabot believed the world was round.
When he heard of the exploit of his fellow-country-
man, and perhaps his fellow-citizen, Christopher
Columbus, proud of Italy, but jealous for Venice,
the republic and city of which he was a naturalized
citizen, Cabot longed also to share in the glory of
new discoveries, and to win the favor of King
Henry VII. Besides romantic notions, his practical
object, like that of all the other navigators, was to
find the lands of jewels and spices, so as to control
the trade in them, if possible, for his sovereign.

King Henry, who took no stock in the project of
Bartholomew Columbus, would take none directly
in Cabot's venture. He was perfectly willing, however, to let the people of Bristol fit out and pay for
any expedition they might send, while he gave his
royal commission to this brilliant Italian.

CHAPTER XI.

IN all human history men are moved as much by sentiment as by matter-of-fact considerations. Now it happened that romance as well as prosaic love of money led to the equipment of the ship *Matthew*, with its total crew of nineteen men, commanded by John Cabot, which sailed from Bristol, England, at sunrise June 24, 1497. This little craft opened a gateway, not for the Italian, but for the English language, people, laws, and ideas, on this American continent. Cabot sailed not only on the Atlantic, but into American history in a way he never dreamed of. On what he did and on what he saw, all subsequent English and British claims to North America were based. Yet he was not seeking the stern reality which he actually met, but a city of fairy tales, an island of legend, the pots of gold that are found only at the roots of a rainbow.

The story runs, that when Tarik the Saracen landed in Portugal and began its conquest, the bishop of Oporto with thousands of his fellow-Christians fled to an island far out in the western Atlantic, where he founded seven cities. This was called Antilia, or the island of the Seven Cities. It was filled with riches of all kinds, even the shore sparkling with golden sands which no one cared for. It was supposed to lie in front of the west of the Cape de Verde group; that is, it was ante-insula or Antilia.

The re-discovery of these islands which had been known to the Romans, by the Portuguese excited a lively interest in Bristol. Every year, between 1484 and 1490, the sailors of Devonshire had made a voyage far westward into the ocean to find the golden strand. After six voyages, the commander of the seventh was to find land.

So, like Jason and the Argonauts in search of the golden fleece, John Cabot pointed his prow toward the setting sun to find Antilia and the Seven Cities, and to take possession of the island of the golden sands for King Henry and England. If not Antilia, he hoped to reach Japan, or China, or spice-lands, or the Golden Chersonese. He sailed due west in the high latitudes, instead of going south to the Cape de Verde Islands. He kept nearer the Arctic Circle than to the Tropic of Cancer.

Very little indeed is known of this voyage. Cabot saw no human being at his landfall some-

where in British America, probably at Cape Breton.
Instead of sparkling gold or cities, he found a bleak
and rocky coast. He landed in what he thought
was the territory of Genghis Khan's successors.
He set up the symbol of the Christian faith, with
the flags of England and Venice — the cross of
St. George and the lion of St. Mark. Being out of
provisions, though fish were amazingly abundant in
the sea, he turned his prow homewards, but over
his larboard he saw two islands.

All that we really know of John Cabot's voyage
is this: some years afterwards, his son Sebastian
Cabot, who may or may not have been with his
father, drew a map and wrote on it: —

" In the year of our Lord 1497, John Cabot, a
Venetian, and his son Sebastian discovered that
country which no one before his time had ventured
to approach, on the 24th of June, about five o'clock
in the morning."

It is not probable that many English people even
as much as heard of this voyage till many years
later, or that the Bristol people set much value
upon the discovery, though King Henry VII. made
the Venetian a present of ten pounds sterling for
finding " the new isle." John Cabot, however, was
called the Grand Admiral. He dressed in silk,
when silk was excessively rare in England. He
maintained a retinue on the streets, and the people

of Bristol ran after him as if he were a second
Columbus. He made a map of his discovery and a
globe which excited interest in England. He died
probably the next year.

Cabot had not found Antilia, but others went
sailing over the seas to reach it. Myths and fairy
tales, which men think true, are long in dying.
We shall see the Spaniards, during the next century, chasing the myth of the Seven Cities among
the Zuñis and their cliff dwellings in New Mexico,
and even among the buffaloes in Kansas. As for
Antilia, the name survives in the Antilles of the
West Indies, of which Cuba is "the pearl."

Sebastian, the second son, nobly took up his
father's work and carried it farther. Believing that
the earth was a globe, he argued that the shortest
path to the dominions of Genghis Khan lay far up
north where the degrees of longitude approached
each other. This young Venetian, in 1498, with a
squadron manned by English volunteers, crossed
the Atlantic. Although it was in July, they could
not set foot on Labrador because of the dense mass
of icebergs. The daylight lasting eighteen hours
was excellent for exploration, and they landed at
many points, noticing that the native dressed in fur
clothing, and had ornaments and tools of copper.
Fish were so plentiful that the ships seemed to
plough their way through them. The bears came

down to the shore and used their claws for grappling hooks, pulling the cod out of the water and feasting on them. The deer were bigger than those in England. He called the country Baccalaos, or codfish land. He sailed somewhere southwardly and then returned home.

There was not much in England at this time to keep an enterprising Italian on her shores, and there was little appreciation anywhere of what the Cabots had done. Sebastian Cabot entered the service of Spain, and made other voyages. He came back to England in 1547, where he made maps and globes, and was chosen president of an English company, organized to trade with Russia through Archangel. He died in London about 1558.

Yet, at such a time the discoveries of the Cabots had no more practical importance than had the voyages of the Norsemen. They could not, in that age and in that era of thought, be of any special benefit to England. They did not, and they could not, produce any special desire for further discoveries; certainly not any for colonization or possession. The rest of the European world was mightily excited over the new regions beyond sea, and book after book on the subject was printed; but in England it was not till 1509, in a funny pamphlet called the "Ship of Fools," that

there was any reference made in English literature
either to Columbus' or to Cabot's wonderful discovery. At that time England was influenced by
Latin ideas in religion, and under the spiritual control of the Pope; and there was no thought of
breaking with his authority, which had been exer-
cised in the division of the earth. For sixty years
the story of the Cabot discoveries was unwritten in
England, and popularly unknown there.

The Pope had already cut the globe into Portuguese and Spanish hemispheres, and any claim of
right founded on discovery must be confirmed by
the Pope, in order to be valid. Few Englishmen
of that day would have thought of disregarding
the Pope's command. Until Latin ideas had been
given up, the yoke of the Pope's authority cast off,
and the people possessed the new world of ideas
that came in with the Reformation, the English
cared little for exploration. Then the proofs of
Cabot's discoveries were used as a sponge to wipe
out the Pope's bull of demarcation, as one erases
chalk writing from a blackboard. When money and
the profits of trade and the fisheries rose clearly
in sight, the English were stirred to conquest
and colonization. This will appear more clearly
in future chapters, when we shall see that, by the
Reformation, all the northern maritime nations
found a new sphere upon the ocean. The sea

became the cradle of the Reformation, and its power was born on the waves.

The time came, in due course, when the pen proved to be mightier than the prow. In 1553, fifty-six years after John Cabot's American landfall, Mr. Richard Eden, who had known the old man, Sebastian Cabot, and seen him die, wrote a little book, "A Treatise on the New India." This roused the English folk to see that their Italian guests, the Cabots, had found a great world for them to conquer and colonize. Eden was a great admirer of the Spaniards, and wanted the English to convert the Indians. He published another book, giving much information from Spanish and other authors about America. He saw Philip II. of Spain and Queen Mary enter London in 1554 on their marriage journey.

Yet not until after the reign of Bloody Mary, and when Elizabeth had long been seated on the throne, and hostilities with Spain begun, did English sailors venture on the deep seas. Then, more than a century after John Cabot's glimpse of Occidental land, the west-country mariners of England sailed the seas over. They made little pretence of discovery or exploration. Their real object was to spoil the Spaniards.

CHAPTER XII.

COLUMBUS had not reached Japan or China, but he still believed he would get there. When Ferdinand and Isabella confirmed him in all his rights and titles, they also authorized the equipment of a new and larger fleet of seventeen vessels, which sailed September 25, 1493. There was nothing to do but sail straight ahead till near the West India Islands. Nearly a month was spent at Porto Rico. When, late in November, they came to the settlement, they found nothing but the bones of their former comrades, who had been unable to maintain authority among themselves or to keep peace with the natives. Selecting a spot thirty miles further east, Columbus founded the first European city in America.

The crew of this second expedition were, for the most part, lazy and avaricious men. Unused to work, they made poor colonists with which to begin an empire. New and strange diseases broke out among them; and even Columbus fell ill. He had written March 14, 1493, before leaving Europe, promising their Invincible Majesties all the gold they needed; but when, in 1494, he was obliged to send home twelve of his ships, instead of lading them with gold or gems, he had only a gloomy report of death, sickness, and woe. Besides this, he made a proposition that African slaves be sent over to labor for the colony. Columbus, neither better nor worse than the men of his age, thus laid the foundation of slavery in America, both of the red and the black man.

Although the merciful King and Queen did not approve of his plan, Columbus had five shiploads of black men from Guinea sent to these new Indies. In the island itself, the natives were conquered by treachery and murder. The Spaniards levied upon the conquered natives a tribute in the form of a hawk's bell full of gold, once in three months, with the alternative, in the case of inability to get the gold, of working like slaves on the farms of their conquerors. The hawk's bell was a tiny measure shaped like a small sleigh-bell, but most of the Indians could not furnish the precious metal, and so were enslaved. This cruel order produced more war, bloodshed, and misery. Within a generation the whole population of Hayti — an island nearly as large as Maine — was swept away through the re-

morseless cruelties of the Spaniards. The coming
of the white man was that of the wolf among
lambs.

In April, 1494, Columbus left the colony to explore unknown lands to the west. On the 12th of
June, just as he thought he was getting near some
great Chinese city full of gold, his men refused to
go any further, and he was obliged to turn back.
But, before he would yield, he compelled eighty of
them to swear that they had touched the continent,
and that it was possible to reach Spain by travelling
westward overland. Whoever, on his return home,
should break his oath was to be heavily fined and
have his tongue cut out. Returning to Hayti, Columbus found that his brother, Bartholomew, had arrived, and that some of the party had seized his ship
and gone home, where they spread very damaging
reports about Christopher. The King, therefore,
sent out an agent, to inquire into affairs, who reached
the colony in October, 1495. Columbus then decided to go home and plead his cause before the
King and Queen. After nearly three years' absence
he reached Cadiz, June 11, 1496.

All went well with the Admiral, while in the presence of Ferdinand and Isabella, who renewed his
commissions and assisted him to fit out a new fleet
of eight ships. It was still very hard to get crews,
for the people of Spain in general were thoroughly

disappointed. Instead of being loaded down with yellow metal, his sailors had brought back yellow faces, made so by strange and awful diseases. Not a little of the wealth imported into Spain was in the form of human flesh, to be sold in Europe as slaves. The street loafers called Columbus the Admiral of Mosquito Land and the man mighty in promises who had done nothing. After long delays, the Admiral was able to secure the required crews by getting the privilege of transporting criminals to the West Indies. Such a policy could not but stamp the very name of colonist and colony with disgrace and ignominy.

It was not until May 30, 1498, that the ships sailed. This time Columbus steered in a southerly course, and his first landfall was at an island with three peaks which he called the Trinity or Trinidad. In our days this island, from its lakes of asphalt, furnishes us with material for roofs and pavements. A few days later, August 1, 1498, Columbus sighted the low land at the mouth of the Orinoco River, and this was most probably the first view of the mainland of America, by Columbus or by any Italian or Spaniard. He noticed the fresh waters rushing out into the salt sea, and called the place the Dragon's Mouth. The land was later called Little Venice, or Venezuela. When the Admiral reached Hayti on the last day of August, both the colony itself and its relation to the natives were at the worst.

Now came melancholy days for Columbus. He got into a quarrel with Francis Roldan, who was ambitious and perhaps treacherous, and whom Columbus finally sent off to Spain with his adherents, each one being allowed a slave or woman. The reports of these men on their arrival added fuel to the fires of detraction already kindled by the enemies of the Genoese of whom so many Spaniards were jealous. A new cargo of slaves added to the irritation felt at Court, and King Ferdinand sent out an officer of his household named Bobadilla, who exceeded his authority, for he sent Columbus home in chains. This was more than the sovereigns had intended. Yet, although they would not again give Columbus command of the island, they gave him another fleet of four ships for further explorations, and agreed to protect his estate.

Still strong in his belief that China or Japan would be his next landfall, the Admiral again started westward. Refused help at Hayti, he sailed on between Cuba and Jamaica, skirting the coast of Central America, and getting into the tornadoes of that region. Among the names he gave, Costa Rica, or the Rich Coast, still holds its own. He explored the rim of the sea and the edge of the land from the Isle of Pines to the east of the Isthmus of Darien, find-

ing some gold, many storms, but no path to Asia.
By August 12, 1503, all his vessels had been wrecked,
and he was left stranded on a barren island, with
a prospect of starvation. His brave companion
Mendez volunteered to reach Hayti in an open
boat, and succeeded. Columbus and his fellow-
survivors, on June 25, 1504, after ten months of
suffering, saw over the waves the relief boats ap-
proaching. A few weeks were spent in the colony.
The battered old man reached Spain after a stormy
voyage, only to find that his best friend Queen Isabella was dead, and that the King now cared very
little for him. He could get no help, and his pite-
ous letters were in vain. He died at Valladolid,
May 20, 1506, but his dust and bones were carried
across the ocean, over which he was the first to sail,
and were deposited in the cathedral of San Domingo,
before the year 1549. In 1796, with imposing ceremonies, their removal to Havana, in Cuba, was
accomplished.

The island on which the first Spanish settlement
in America began, later passed into the control of
France, and then after revolution became the seat
of the negro republics, Hayti and San Domingo.
President Grant was once eager to have the United
States purchase San Domingo, but the sentiment
of our country was so strong against him that the
project was abandoned. In course of time all the

Spanish possessions in America, except Cuba, were
lost to Spain.

Painfully and miserably, Christopher Columbus
gained the aureole of immortal fame. Before he
died, about seven thousand miles of the coast of
the double continent had been discovered and
mapped. During his life, Hispaniola was the chief
seat of gold production in these western lands,
and from 1492 to 1510, five hundred thousand
ducats of gold were sent to Spain from this place ;
whence also the hammock was introduced into
Europe. Peter Martyr, as early as 1494, spoke of
a " new world," though yet a very little one. Commerce between the lately explored Africa and the
newly discovered America was almost wholly in
human flesh and blood.

It was not only an Italian from Spain who first
steered westward, and discovered the West Indian
archipelago and South America, an Italian and
his son from England, who sighted islands and
coasts in the ice-regions of North America, an
Italian in Italy who divided the world in half and
gave it away, but the whole double continent of
America bears an Italian name. Amerigo Vespucci was a Florentine, born for trade rather than
for learning, March 9, 1451. The boy Amerigo
was educated by his uncle, a Dominican monk. In
the business house of the great merchant princes,

Medici, he found employment until the failure of the Eastern trade. Then went to Cadiz. Later, he was employed by another Florentine named Berandi, and helped in preparing Columbus' second expedition in 1493. When Berandi, who had taken a royal contract to fit out another fleet, died, Vespucci stepped forward and fulfilled the contract.

Vespucci kept up an interest in his old home, and wrote letters to the chief magistrate of Florence. All we know about the travels in the westward world, of America's godfather, are from translations of these letters which perhaps have long ago perished. We gather from them that Vespucci made four voyages, each beginning in May, and that two of them, in 1497 and 1499, were for the King of Spain, Vespucci acting probably as pilot or factor. With four ships, in the first expedition, he says that he reached land, "upon a coast which we thought to be that of a continent, which many think to be the northern coast of South America." This would bring him within sight of the American continent, several weeks earlier than Cabot's landfall, and fourteen months before Columbus caught sight of South America at the Orinoco.

However, Vespucci never claimed the honor of the discovery of the double continent, or of naming the Americas. How America came to be this Italian's namesake happened in a curious way. In

1507, the year after Columbus died, at the college in the little French town Saint Die, was a German teacher of geography named Martin Waldseemüller, who published his lecture notes in a Latin pamphlet entitled "An Introduction to a Description of the World." To this booklet of a few pages, a copy of which is now worth its weight in gold, he added translations into Latin of Vespucci's letters. He also wrote, "The Fourth part of the world having been discovered by Americus, it may be called Amerige; that is, the land of Americus or America." These letters were widely read, for Latin was the one tongue common to all educated people in Europe. Thus, this German, whose countrymen had so little to do with the discovery of America, — though afterward a good deal to do with the making of it, — gave the new world a name that stuck to it.

Though applied at first only to the South American continent, just as Asia was originally only the name of a province, it soon became that of the whole land-mass between the poles.

Vespucci was a friend of Columbus, and probably had no idea of taking away any glory from him or from Cabot. In 1515, after Vespucci had been dead three years, and the idea that the earth was round had become quite common, the German, Schooner, made his famous globe. This is the way the world then looked to the Europeans: we see the name

America applied to the South American continent.
Something is known, also, of the mainland lying
north, but it is not yet called North America.
There is plenty of sea or vacant space above the
latitude of Labrador. Westward, Japan, as a single
long island, is apparently but a few miles off. Still
further to the Occident, upper India projects out
within a short distance of Japan. If the Italians
discovered, the Germans named, America. A large
portion of the northern part of South America was
later explored by Germans, to whom the Emperor
Charles V., in 1529, leased the province of Venezuela as security for a loan of money. For a century
or so, Germans and Spaniards were on a mad hunt
for that American will-of-the-wisp, *El hombre dorado*,
or the gilded man.

Only gradually did the real idea of a "new world,"
and of a great continent lying between Europe and
China, get into the heads of the people of Europe.
America was yet very far from being fully discovered.
Certainly its real character was not known. Even if
they talked about a "new world," they meant simply
some western coasts and islands newly discovered.
It was reserved for a Portuguese, who afterwards
became a naturalized Spaniard, to be the real discoverer of America not merely at one or two points,
but as a continent by itself, and a very large obstacle
in the way to China, while one of his ships actually

sailed around the globe, being the first to circum-
navigate it.

It is true that the western side of North America
was revisited by Drake, the Englishman, after the
Spaniards had seen and sailed along it, and that
after Magellan, much remained still to be discovered.   Indeed, much of the North American continent, whose northern end is still unknown, even now
remains to be explored.   We cannot yet say whether
the North Pole is in the water or on the land.

Magellan was a boy about thirteen years old when
he first heard of the triumphs of Columbus.   From
his twenty-fifth to his thirty-second year he accompanied those Portuguese ships which sailed clear
into the Malay Archipelago, and among the Spice
Islands.   While fighting the Moors in Morocco, in
1514, he first thought out the plan of getting through
America in order to find China; for Balboa's discovery had shown that there was an ocean beyond.
Because his own government, as he thought, had
treated him badly, and would not aid him, he applied
to Spain, and became a Spanish citizen.   Reaching
the splendid city of Seville in October, 1517, he
lived in the house of an exiled Portuguese, Diego
Barboza, a man of position and influence, whose
daughter he married.   There, amid the groves
of oranges, lemons, and olives he awaited his
opportunity.

The young Netherlander, born in Ghent, who became the great Emperor Charles V., was now King of Spain, and he looked kindly upon young Magellan's scheme to tap the riches of the Chinas and the Indies. Bishop Fonseca, who had opposed Columbus, Balboa, and Cortez, was also warmly interested. Magellan's proposal was to take a Spanish fleet to the Malay Archipelago over a new route. At this time the Portuguese were trading directly with India and the Spice Islands by an all-sea route around Africa. The Court of Lisbon protested, and tried to prevent Magellan's expedition by offering him and his friends brilliant inducements to return to Portugal. Magellan was warned to keep clear of that half of the world belonging to Portugal, but he expected to reach the other spice regions, which were inside the Spanish meridian, by sailing westward. A rich merchant joined him and offered to go on private speculation, but Charles V. finally sent out at government expense five ships, which swung clear of their moorings at San Lucas September 20, 1519.

Touching at Madeira, trading with the Indians on the Brazilian coast, exploring the Rio de la Plata, following the unknown coast of Patagonia, he reached, March 31, the port of San Julian, where a mutineer was hanged. Magellan decided to remain here till finer weather came on. Leaving late in August, he discovered, on October 21, the day holy to the Eleven Thousand Virgins, the strait which he called after St. Ursula and her throng of martyr maidens, " Todos Los Santos." He sent in two ships to explore the inlet, but they could find no end to it; as it is over three hundred miles long. So, thinking that he had discovered the passage to China, Magellan ordered the whole fleet through. They spent a month at the work, stopping often to fish or explore. Reaching the open ocean November 28, Magellan called it " Pacific," or the peaceful sea, on account of the fine weather. This strait has ever since been a well-travelled highway. It was named " Magellan " by the Spaniards, Cape Virgin and Cape Holy Spirit being at each entrance.

Magellan now steered for the north. His men suffered greatly from bad food and water, which brought on scurvy, that ancient enemy of the sailor. From this disease seafaring men have suffered for ages, until toward the middle of this century, when onions and other vegetables, lime-juice and anti-scorbutics have routed the enemy, and driven it to exile, so that now a case of scurvy is rarely seen on board a well-kept ship. At one of the islands, natives stole one of his boats, so he gave the group a name which still sticks, — " Ladrones," or Robber Islands. Not correctly informed as to the position of the Moluccas, his ships kept too far north; but on March 16, 1521, he discovered Samar, one of the group of islands named — though not till some years later — after Philip II. of Spain, and called " Philippines." The chief of one island was very hospitable, and, as the Spaniards thought, formally accepted allegiance to Spain; but at Mactan Island the natives were hostile, and in his attack upon them, April 27, 1521, the commander and eight of his men were killed.

Magellan could afford to die. He had discovered the southwest passage to China. The voyage, however, was continued, and one of the ships reached Spain. The captain was honored by the King with a coat of arms, on which was a globe, with the motto, "You first sailed round Me." A Spanish expedition under Villalobos was soon afterwards sent out, and took possession of the islands so wonderfully rich in timber, metals, gums, and spices.

CHAPTER XIII.

A S with the discoveries of Cabot and the Norsemen, so with Magellan's. The importance of
his voyaging was not at first recognized. The mind
of Europe was bent on finding the direct passage
to the old gold and spice lands of Asia, while
America was ever the undesirable obstacle in the
way. For eighty years or more to come, men kept
on trying to drive their ships through this barrier,
hoping to find some river, bay, strait, or other water
passage through America in order to reach Japan
and China. Nevertheless, geographers began to
divide the Indies, to distinguish between the "East"
and the "West" Indies.

One thing healed the smart of the Spaniards' disappointment, while it kept them from making any
further important explorations in North America.
This was the discovery of mines of gold and silver
in Mexico and Peru, together with the treasures
won by seizure. Nevertheless, in time the great
thought and practical achievement of Magellan
bore fruit. He had given the first distinct knowl-

edge of the Pacific. As the Spaniards had discovered the Philippines, which were far enough around the world to be reckoned outside of the Portuguese claim, Villalobos and his men soon colonized them.

This group of over four hundred islands, between Formosa and the Moluccas, forming the northern part of the Malay Archipelago, with an area of one hundred and fifteen thousand square miles, an exceedingly fertile soil rich in products both natural and cultivated, without dangers of wild beasts, and valuable in every way, became the rich treasure house of the King of Spain in the far East, while Peru and Mexico remained his inexhaustible storehouse in the West.

The Spaniards in America had little taste for work, but much for adventure. Most of them preferred robbery to earning an honest living. They did not even care to mine the precious metals, but chose rather to roam over the continent and to lay their hands on gold wherever it had been already stored up.

Once, an American popular lecturer went to Great Britain for pounds, shillings, and pence. "How strange," said Sandy, Taffy, and John, — one and all, — "we thought America was the place to make money." "True," replied the lecturer; "but here it is made already."

So with the Spaniards, they wanted gold already dug and refined. Furthermore, they hid their purpose under the garb of religion. It is a curious fact, also, that South America was explored and its geography gradually learned because the Spaniards kept chasing phantoms and echoes. The myth of the El Dorado lured them on. What was this?

In Venezuela, or Little Venice, there are many lakes, in each of which the Indians thought that a god dwelt who must be worshipped with offerings of gold or precious stones. Herein they were like the old Japanese, who believed in the Queen of the World and her palaces under the sea. On the top of a little mountain near Santa Fé, was one lake, at the bottom of which there lived a goddess, in whose honor a wonderful ceremony had been observed from times long before the coming of the Spaniards, and until about 1490. It was this: Whenever a new war-chief was chosen, there was a great parade of the warriors to the lake. In front walked a band of mourners, who were naked men painted red. These were followed by others, richly decorated with gold and emeralds, with feather crowns or with jaguars' skins. Their music was made with horns, pipes, and conch shells. The priests wore tall black caps and black robes marked with white crosses. The elders, nobles, and higher priests carried the newly chosen chief, the gilded

man, on a platform hung with sheets of gold. This
living man was clothed with pure gold. His body
had been first smeared all over with resinous gum,
and then fine gold dust was powdered over him,
until, from crown to sole, he was shining like a
golden statue.

The procession halted at the water's edge. Then
the chief and his bearers stepped upon a raft, and in
the presence of thousands of spectators pushed out
to the middle of the lake. There the chieftain
plunged into the water and washed off his covering
of gold, while his tribesmen threw in the gems and
jewellery they had brought with them. Dancing
and music closed the exercises of the day. All this
was meant as an offering to propitiate the goddess
that dwelt in the lake.

This ceremony was of the same nature as the
offerings made by the Iroquois Indians, when passing Rock Regio or Split Rock in Lake Champlain,
where Arendt van Curler was drowned. Only, the
northern savages threw in tobacco, a pipe, or some
similar gifts to placate the god residing there. Perhaps gold dust was of no more value to the native
Venezuelans of A.D. 1490 than was tobacco to the
Mohawks.

In digging for drains in Venezuela, men have
found, besides other interesting metallic relics, a
group of ten golden human figures representing

the raft with the gilded chief and his companions.

When the Spaniards first heard the story of the
chieftain clothed in gold, — *el hombre dorado*, as it
is in Spanish, — they were too late. It was "the
day after the fair." The Muysca Indians near
Bogota having conquered the tribe whose chief was
the El Dorado, or the gilded, the ceremony had
ceased twenty years or more before white men
heard the story.

When the fact died, the myth was born, even as
the western clouds take on their most gorgeous
colors after the sun has set. Nevertheless, for
nearly a hundred years, the myth survived the
reality on which it had been founded. The Spaniards and the Germans went all over the northern
half of South America, searching for the phantom,
which was not laid until the Germans Von Hum-
boldt and Schomburgh and Bandelier, in our century, showed the beginning and growth of the
delusion.

Both stories — that of the Grand Khan and that
of the Gilded Chieftain — had already changed from
fact to fiction, from history to mythology, when the
Italians and Spaniards began to chase them. The
" dead fact stranded on the shores of the oblivious
years" was like the coal tar which, in its decompo-
sition turns into gorgeous aniline colors, and tints

the river current with iridian splendors. Nevertheless, because of this lust for gold and the spirit of
adventure, the new continent was opened on all
sides.

Not at first, but in due time, the Strait of Magellan became a practical highway. Commerce between Mexico and the Philippines developed. The
Japanese Christians, who had come under direction
of their new Spanish missionary teachers, to visit
Europe to declare themselves spiritual vassals of
the Holy See at Rome, to do obeisance to the
King of Spain, and to leave splendid gifts of armor
and weapons at Madrid, sailed by way of the Pacific
and crossed through Mexico. Returning home,
these Japanese had gone entirely around the globe.
In a very large sense of the word, the sovereign of
Spain was " King of the Indies."

Here, in our story of achievement, which eventu-
ated in the settlement and appearance in history of
the United States of America, practically ends the
history of the Spanish discoveries in American
coasts and waters, so far as we are directly con-
cerned. The Portuguese colonized Brazil, and the
Spaniards discovered and occupied the other portions of South America, as well as most of the
West India Islands, Central America, and Florida.
The Confederacies of Indian tribes in Mexico and
Peru were conquered, and those countries were

made Spanish provinces from which poured silver rivers into the treasury at Madrid. As many provinces were added by Cortez to the realm of the Emperor Charles V., as his father had had cities.

The Spaniards also made persistent and important explorations in what is now the southern part of our country, especially in the Cotton States, from Florida to the Mississippi, and in the southwestern regions from Texas to California. We shall glance at these later.

Though not evident to the world at the time, when one of Magellan's squadron circumnavigated the globe, it is now clear in the perspective of history that some Power had determined that America in the North Temperate Zone, its best portion as to climate, fertility, mineral wealth, and natural highways, was to be occupied and dominated by other than the Latin races. Italy owned not a foot of soil. Portugal had only sub-tropical Brazil. Spain held, drained, and looted lower North America, Central America, and most of South America. It was reserved for the northern nations of Europe only partially to discover and to explore, but wholly to occupy and colonize the territory now comprising the United States of America.

When America had been known as a continent, and the world first circumnavigated, there was little sign that the English, Dutch, or Scandinavian would

launch out into the deep, or sail their ships beyond
sight of land. It was the Reformation that gave
England her sea power and Holland her eastern
empire, and which made America the nobler theatre
of the enterprise and faith of the Teutonic peoples.
The Japanese Yoshitsuné, the Mongols, and the
Turks, by pushing westward, not only sent the
southern nations of Christendom out on the sea in
quest of lands beyond the Atlantic, but, by driving
the Greek scholars with the Greek New Testament
among Germanic nations, helped unconsciously the
Reformation, the Dutch Republic, English sea-
power, and the United States of America.

CHAPTER XIV.

FRANCE is one of the maritime European nations that has a large ocean front and a coast population which, from ancient times, has been daring upon the sea. While her southern neighbors were inquiring about new routes to those sunny Oriental lands where French crusaders had won immortal fame, the French could not remain indifferent. Every man of public spirit in southern Europe seemed to be talking of new sea-routes to the gold and spice lands. Being a people strongly inclined to Latin Christianity, the French needed fish dinners, at least three days in a week, and their sailors went far and wide to find the material.

When King Francis I. heard how the Pope had carved the world in half, for only two nations living in one peninsula, he demanded to see Father Adam's will. He doubted the right of an Italian prince to dispose of so much of the universe by means of a bull. When the bold fisherman of St. Malo sailed far to the west, and, quite probably, fished off the banks of Newfoundland, the King was glad to hear reports about a possible New France towards the setting sun.

Yet, it is not probable that any French national ship with a French commander saw the North American continent until after an Italian navigator from Florence came in person and interested the French King and Court in his plans for a voyage westward. Verrazano, as his name was, had travelled in Greece and Syria, making money in the spice and silk trade. When forced by Turkish successes to look elsewhere, he did so. He took the advice which old Italians then frequently gave to their juniors, — "Go west, young man." He entered the French naval service in 1505, when twenty-five years old. Twelve years afterwards, he sailed to the East Indies in a Portuguese vessel, becoming an expert navigator. Again, in a French privateer, he waylaid Spanish ships coming from the West Indies, capturing one in 1523, which contained the spoils which Cortez had taken from Montezuma in Mexico. After that, he thought he should like to see the silver continent for himself.

The next year, 1524, he went out on a voyage of exploration to North America, making landfall near Cape Fear. He sailed northward along the coast, discovering a bay which was either that of New York or Narragansett. Then going four hundred and fifty miles northeast, to latitude 50°, he returned

to France. From Dieppe, July 19, 1524, he wrote
to the King, claiming to have discovered over two
thousand miles of a new coast. Once again, he got
already to sail over the Atlantic either as a merchant to the Indies, or as a corsair for the pillage
of Spanish vessels, but his career closed inglori-
ously. He was captured on the southern coast of
Spain and was put to death as a pirate.

Indeed, not a few of the first discoverers, now so
famous, suffered similar varieties of fate. They
were thrown into prison, kept in chains, or had
their heads cut off. Instead of winning gold,
princes' favors, glory, and honor, they found themselves and their children disgraced. Frequently in
those days, between discoverers and explorers and
pirates and sea-rovers, there was but a thin, sometimes invisible, line of difference.

It seems astonishing, in our day, that with so
many famous names, as those of John Cabot, Verrazano, and others, we find so little written or
printed evidence of their work. Yet there seems
little doubt but that this Venetian made such a
voyage, and that he discovered new coasts in
America. His fame rests upon a publication of
Ramusio, who was the secretary of the senate in
Venice. Besides publishing Verrazano's letter in
1556, and attempting to popularize in Italy his
brother's fame as a discoverer, Ramusio may have

embellished the story, besides adding that Verrazano made another voyage to America and was
killed by the savages. Ramusio knew the Cabots,
and was one of the first to collect and publish
accounts of voyages and travels.

Thus it would seem that the first of French discoveries in America were made by another of those
ubiquitous Italians in foreign employ. The Italians
then led the world in nautical science and in daring
on the sea.

Nevertheless, Verrazano's discoveries had no
more immediate practical importance among the
French than had those of the Cabots among the
English, until Jacques Cartier entered the river St.
Lawrence and began New France. Cartier was
born in that little fishing-village named St. Malo,
the fortified seaport town on the English Channel,
near the mouth of the Rance River, from which
brave adventurous fishermen had probably sailed,
even before his time, to the fishing-banks off Newfoundland. Like their English brethren of the
sea, the brave sailors of St. Malo hated the Inquisition and paid back the Spaniards in their own coin,
when the latter were too zealous to reduce heretics
to ashes.

To this day thousands of French fishermen come
to the Grand Banks to catch cod. Not infrequently
their little boats are cut in two and sunk, by the

ocean steamers that rush through the waters like
railway trains.   Crossing the Atlantic in September,
1895, for the eighth time, I remember that our
steamer made a detour in order to avoid a wreck
which had been caused by collision.   The gunwale
of this single-masted smack had been stove in, but
the stump of the mast remained.   The seaweed
had already gathered, and the hulk had become a
"derelict."   As our big ship got in her rear, I read
through my glass, on the stern of the waterlogged
wreck, " Jacinth, Saint Malo."

Cartier was born on the last day of 1594, and followed the sea from boyhood.   Like many other
young men of his century, he hoped some day to
find the western passage to China.   When the war
between Spain and France was over, and the privateers had to seek new employment, Cartier was
given two ships, of fifty tons each, and 162 picked
men.   Leaving St. Malo April 20, 1534, he sailed
straight across the ocean.   He sighted the headlands of Newfoundland on May 10th, meeting
storms, floating ice, white bears, and wild fowls,
seemingly as numerous as snowflakes in a winter's
storm.   His men explored the island coasts, and
straits, and landing, they set up a cross.   At one
place they found a French ship from Brest.   This
was not surprising, for at various points these coasts
had been visited by the Norsemen, by Cabot, by

CARTIER SETS UP A CROSS IN NEWFOUNDLAND.

Cortereal the Portuguese, by Basque whalers, and by fishermen from Brittany. Probably hundreds of vessels had been off the banks for fish before Cartier came.

They thought that Labrador, which the Norsemen had named the country of slate or rock, was the land of Nod, to which Cain had been banished, and indeed the natives whom they met seemed to have Cain's bad manners. The red man's opinions of the Frenchmen are not given. They kept on amid mists and storms, examining the archipelago, and sprinkling the names of the saints very frequently upon promontories and harbors. Not till the last day in June did they reach the mainland. The Micmac Indians came around the ship in such numbers that Cartier was obliged to fire blank cartridges out of his cannon to scare them away. The next day he landed, and pleased their chief with the present of a red hat. He met other Indians, but having no provisions to spare, could not safely stay longer. He turned his prows homeward August 15, having two Indians on board. On this voyage he found neither the mouth of the St. Lawrence River nor the route to Japan. His Indians, with their curious costumes, and hair done up like a bundle of hay, with feathers sticking in the mass, made a great sensation in France. They certainly helped to stir up interest in further explorations.

The next year, the King, wishing to see more of his new subjects, and to hear of new realms, gave Cartier three ships in which to seek further for some waterway across America to spice lands; but the St. Malo sailors, not caring to venture again where they found only icebergs, white bears, birds, codfish, and red savages, were slow in signing articles. They thought the whole scheme was wild, and Cartier a dreamer. So Cartier had to man his ships with pardoned criminals, though some very good sailors went with him. During July and August he met with the same stormy weather as before, and was totally discouraged in not finding a passage through to the Pacific Ocean. Two Indians told him that the strait between Anticosti and Salvador, which he had named St. Peter's Channel, led to a river which narrowed inland and became shallow, besides having rapids. This river, they said, was the entrance to Canada.

When, on August 18, Cartier saw many whales driving westward, he being too full of the Chinese idea to believe the Indians, ordered the ships to move west. Soon he came to water that was first brackish and then fresh. Nevertheless, having China on the brain, he thought that even fresh water might lead to regions of spice and silk. Soon he came into the broad river, passed the Saguenay, and in mid-September reached the site of Quebec.

Canada, ever rich in forests, was then lovely with the colors of the frost-touched leaves, and seemed almost like heaven to the weary Frenchman. How the country got its name is still a puzzle. Some say the gold-seeking Spaniards had seen the country and cried out in disgust, "Aca! nada" — "Nothing there." Others derive the name from the Iroquois word *kannata*, meaning a collection of huts or a village.

The new-comers made friends with the Indians, who gathered in thousands to see the ships; but Donnacona, then chief, not liking Cartier's proposed exploration of the river, tried to frighten the white men away with the antics of some of his tribesmen dressed like imps. These, he said, were messengers from the god that dwelt farther up the river and who did not like strangers. At such painted and tricked-out demons, Cartier, who was familiar with European painted and sculptured devils, was only amused. With a party of men he went on his way, exploring the river as far as the rapids. Landing at one point, Cartier and his party climbed the high ground, enjoyed the splendid view, and called the name of the place Montreal, the royal hill, King's Mountain. After an astonishing amount of religious ceremonies, the white men ended with theft and treachery. It was a slave-catching and a slave-stealing age, when neither English, Spanish, Dutch,

nor French had any conscience about burning men
for holding different religious opinions, depriving
dark-skinned men of their liberty, or of killing
"infidels," and Cartier seized and carried off several
of the Indian leaders, including Donnacona.

After a winter spent at the harbor of the Holy
Cross, with much suffering from scurvy, of which they
were cured by drinking decoctions of the leaves and
bark of the white pine, the Frenchmen returned to
St. Malo, July 1, 1536. The King was delighted to
see his new subjects, to hear of Cartier's success,
and to learn of the great river St. Lawrence. Nothing, however, was done until 1541, when Cartier
sailed again with Roberval and five ships. This
time, having encountered weather even more stormy
than before, little was accomplished beyond exploring the rapids above Montreal. When he got
home, his king knighted Cartier. From this time
forth, fleets of French fishing-vessels crossed the
Atlantic regularly, and Portuguese, Spanish, and
French vessels brought thousands of tons of cod
for Friday food to Europe.

France had now solid ground for claims upon,
and further occupation of, America. Nevertheless,
there were no immediate movements towards
Canada. The French were soon after disturbed by
internal dissensions and wars for the freedom of
conscience. Catherine de Medici, who was the real

ruler of the kingdom during the reign of her three
sons, did not care to spend her resources or attempt
to get new revenues in the scarcely known regions
beyond the Atlantic.

Aside from some minor enterprises and failures
in Canada, the only French attempts during the
sixteenth century to colonize any part of North
America were made during the struggle of the
Huguenots for freedom in religion. By the advice
of Admiral Coligny, Jean Ribaut took out twenty
or thirty settlers and built a little log fort at Port
Royal, in what is now South Carolina. Finding
grapes plentiful, they gathered and pressed them,
making about twenty hogsheads of wine; but in
that lonesome land, between the forest wilderness
and the sea, when winter came on, they nearly died
of homesickness. Resolving to return home, they
built a rude boat out of green timber, for which
they made sails and rigging from their bed-clothes
and clothing, and then turned their prow eastward.
Wonderful to relate, they were seen by a ship,
picked up, and taken to England.

A second expedition was sent out the next year,
1564, under Laudonnière. This time the French
built a fort further south, on the St. John's River,
in Florida, where, after a while, they were reinforced by Jean Ribaut, who came with seven ships
and three hundred men. These Huguenot settle-

ments represented the efforts of Admiral Coligny
and his fellow-patriots to found a French Protestant state in America.

How real the Pope's division of the world was
then held to be, and how terrible it then was to
break his command, Coligny and Ribaut soon discovered. The King of Spain sent one of his
bravest officers, Pedro Menendez, to uproot the
settlement. The Spaniard arrived with a great
fleet and force. By a clever ambuscade he surprised the French garrison, captured the women
and children alive, and massacred the men found in
the fort. He then induced Ribaut, whose fleet had
been nearly ruined by storms, with three hundred
of his followers, who were almost starved, to sur-
render on the promise of protection. The prisoners
were then marched off to the Spanish settlements
in Florida, near St. Augustine, and there were all
deliberately shot in cold blood, for in those days
Spaniards did not keep faith with men called
heretics.

The King of France, being a true follower of
the Pope, paid no attention either to this insult to
his flag or to the massacre of his subjects, but
a French nobleman named de Gourgues, at his
own expense, sailed with ships and men to Florida
to take revenge. He surprised and captured the
Spanish garrison, and hanged every one of the

prisoners, putting above each an inscription on a board, " Not Spaniards, but Assassins." Unable with his force to attack St. Augustine, he sailed away, and the Spaniards were left in possession of the country.

How far away seem these days, when human beings killed each other in the name of Christ and thought they were doing God service! But slowly have men learned that the Almighty is not honored by those who cloak their murderous passions under the name of religion. All churches were then political, and therefore persecuted those who held the doctrine of the separation of Church and State, now the law of the United States of America. Yet already in Europe, from Switzerland to England, the believers in the right of Christians to govern themselves without politicians, native or foreign, were sowing the seed of those truths which have become flower and fruit in the Constitution and laws of the United States.

L

LIKE the horns of the crescent enclosing the old moon, the United States projects far south around the Gulf of Mexico. On the west is the southern boundary of Texas, and the warm water is salt until it touches the fresh flood of the Rio Grande. On the east there projects southward, Florida, a land reared for the most part out of the ocean by coral insects, yet with its highlands and orange plantations, its coquina or shell-rock, and its Everglades. In both of these southern extremities of our country there are many Spanish names, among which those of the saints abound. From the frequent references to dogmas and mysteries of the Christian faith in French and Spanish names, one would imagine that the people of these countries were religious above all others, but this does not follow.

St. Augustine, the oldest town in the United States, was founded by the Spaniards. Florida and all the land in what is now the Cotton States, as far west as the Mississippi, were first explored by men

of Castile and Aragon. The whole country across
to California was traversed by heroes from the same
kingdom, whose names, whose blood, whose architecture and religion still attest their courage and
enterprise and show how deeply they have made
their mark upon the history of our country.

Florida is the first of the states of our Union
that was ever seen by a European. It was visited
as one would visit a fairyland, to find the pot of gold
under the rainbow, or the golden fleece before the
dragon's shrine. Herein we see mental differences
between the southern and the northern nations of
Europe. The former are more romantic. They act
oftener upon ideas alone. The northern peoples
are more practical and prosaic. The Spaniards, in
many instances, went to America under dreamy
delusions and with chivalrous ideas, chasing myths
and shadows. Their brains were full of old-world
notions and fairy tales, which they tried to realize
on this side of the Atlantic. No wonder they laid
themselves open to the wit and sarcasm of Cervan-
tes, who poked fun at the hare-brained knights
charging at windmills when other objects of attack
were absent. The Spaniards explored America not
only for gold but to realize all sorts of fancies that
now belong to fairyland and the Arabian Nights.
The more practical Englishmen and Dutchmen
cared next to nothing about the new continent in

the west, until they saw there was good soil, fish, mines, and money in it, and opportunity to make fortunes.

There was no more strange quest in Teutonic or Japanese fairy world than was that of the gray-bearded knight of Aragon, who had heard of a miraculous fountain whose waters would make old people young again. This was one of those wonderful myths of the middle ages, which came from the far East, and thence through the Moors to Europe, and which the Spaniards really brought with them across the sea. In the new world they tried to see what their eyes were looking for. They had expected to find that part of the old world, which is as wonderful in its myths as in its realities, — China and Japan. For a hundred years after Columbus, they never thought of any "new" world although they were actually in it. They brought with them the Chinese and Arabic notions of alchemy, the philosopher's stone, the elixir of life, the fountain of youth, the Amazons, the odd notions of Chinese Tauism, and the myth of the Seven Cities. To these they added new American myths, like that of The Gilded Man, which not for hundreds of years were entirely given up. Even yet, lingering among the uneducated, we catch glimpses of their ghosts in old romances, in gypsy lore, in almanacs, and in fortune-tellers' advertisements. Yet these notions once moved thousands of men to cross the seas, traverse deserts, jungles, and swamps, and to starve and die in American forests.

Ponce de Leon opened his eyes in Aragon, in 1460. Of noble family, he grew up to be a soldier. He helped to wrest Granada from the Moors, and went with Columbus, in 1493, to found the city of Little Spain. At fifty years of age, he was made governor of Porto Rico. One day he heard, from a native, of an island to the northwest, called Dimini, which had a miraculous spring into which if an old man plunged, he would come out without wrinkles and gray hair, and be strong once more. This news set the old man's imagination on fire. He became as eager for the plunge in the forest fountain, as was Don Quixote to charge the windmill.

Receiving his sovereign's permission to investigate and settle Dimini, Ponce de Leon sailed in March, 1513. He discovered some of the Bahama Islands, and in the lovely month of April, on Easter Sunday, he landed a few miles north of St. Augustine. Taking possession with great ceremony, he called the land Pascua Florida, or the Paschal Flowery Land, the first word being the Spanish for Pascal or Palm Sunday. Curiously enough, the China so long sought for by voyagers from Europe, is also called the Flowery Land, or, in Spanish La Florida. Ponce de Leon sailed down the coast

about two hundred miles, and then returned to his
island.   There he was kept busy for several years
by those Indian wars, in which the aborigines were
exterminated.   At last, in 1521, he went again with
three ships and with soldiers to conquer the new
country, and get his baptism of youth.   In attempting to plant a colony, instead of finding a fountain
of life he was met by hostile Indians, and so badly
wounded that he died soon after reaching Cuba.
The first flowers of Spanish history in Florida were
those of nightshade rather than of amaranth.

Florida, which meant to a Spaniard any and all
land north of the Gulf of Mexico, having been discovered, the next step was to colonize it.   For this
purpose, the King of Spain sent out a splendid fleet
of vessels with six hundred men, under the command of de Narvaez.   The treasurer was Cabeza
de Vaca, of whom we shall hear again.   He was
born in the town of Xeres, of which "sherry" wine
is the namesake, and he became the greatest of
early American travellers.   He was the Stanley of
Darkest America, known in its interior less than we
now know, in some respects at least, the planet Mars.

Instead of landing on the east coast, the little
army, reduced by mutiny to about four hundred
men, reached a place near Tampa Bay, probably at
Clearwater Harbor, on the west coast.   Landing was
effected on Good Friday, in the year 1528.   While

the soldiers marched inland and northward, the sailors in their fleet followed along the coast.

The explorers met with misfortunes from the very first. Expecting to live off the land, the hungry men found no food, but everywhere encountered fiercely hostile Indians. Then began a long war. Out of every canebrake and from every swamp, sped the deadly arrows.

In their wild fastnesses, the Florida savages, loving their oozy lair, long defied the white man's prowess. During our century, these Seminoles ambuscaded Colonel Dade and his brave band of over one hundred men. Even yet the swamps of the Everglades are not fully explored.

An advance in the hot weather in ancient Florida must have been a frightful task. Loaded down with their armor, weapons, and clumsy firearms, the Spaniards floundered about among the rivers, lakes, and swamps, making, with their gay dress and shining breastplates and helmets, splendid targets for their foes. They were quickly decimated by the agate-tipped shafts of their unseen enemies, and by starvation. Worse than all was their lack of unity. Losing morals and discipline, one set plotted against the other.

When they reached the coast, they were unable to find their ships. With tremendous labor, they built five miserable boats and sailed westward along

the coast line of the Gulf hoping to reach Mexico.
Terrible storms swooped down upon them. The
miserable craft were scattered and wrecked. The
castaways found themselves on a strange shore
beyond the mouth of the Mississippi River, with
starvation facing them. In order to preserve life,
they had to turn cannibals. The shores of the
wretched island which they called Mal Hodo, or
Misfortune Island, were inhabited by poorly fed
savages who kept body and soul together with
roots, berries, clams, and fish, from the sea, but
who, nevertheless, treated the white men kindly.
Without weapons or clothing, which had been lost
in the water, the Spaniards spent the winter on the
island. In the spring thirteen of the sixteen survivors tried to escape, but were captured and all
killed except three, who were kept as slaves.

Of the great expedition there remained but four
half-starved sick men, one of whom was the now
famous Cabeza de Vaca, the first man to traverse
the North American continent, as we shall see.
His name means Cow-Head, but he had the brains
of an unusually bright man. In the Norse mythology, the cow was the primal animal of creation,
and the cow's head at the prow of the Norseman's
galley first pointed to the new world. So also this
Spaniard, honorably named after the head of a cow,
was, in a threefold sense, a remarkable man. He

was the first pioneer who explored the whole southern part of the United States. He was the first
American commercial traveller, the forerunner of
the great and worthy host of to-day. He was the
founder of the Cherokee theology, and told his
savage friends the story of the creation, at which,
two centuries later, the American missionaries in
Georgia and the theologians at Andover were
greatly puzzled, because Cherokee tradition so
closely resembled the Hebrew narrative.

We must not forget that these were the first
Europeans to look upon the Mississippi; for in
their voyage westward, they had passed the great
fresh water current which rushes into the Gulf of
Mexico. Their Island of Misfortune was west of
the great river, probably at Matagorda Bay, in
Texas. At any rate, they were so far from Florida
that they neither heard of the next explorer of
Florida nor did he hear of them.

Leaving Cabeza de Vaca for a while, we shall
anticipate a little by continuing the story of the
further exploration of Florida.

The results of the great expedition had not been
cheering. No doubt, in Spain, many a jibe was
made at the flowery name first given to what proved
to be a land of storms and disaster. Nevertheless, there were young Spaniards ever ready to
dare and to do for sovereign and country, especially

when gold had been already so quickly gained elsewhere, and honors so quickly showered upon certain
of their countrymen in other fields.   One example,
among many, of quick success was that of the
Spanish student, Ferdinand de Soto, who, when
but twenty-three years old, came to the new world.
He was with Balboa in his discovery of the Pacific,
and with Pizarro in Peru.   Then he returned to
Spain a wealthy man, with a name as well as a
fortune, and was able to get for his wife the
daughter of his noble friend who had helped him
in the days of youth and poverty.   When only
forty years old, he was rich enough to lend money
to the Emperor Charles V., but he longed for still
greater glory.   Hearing Cabeza de Vaca's story of
the Zuñi tribes of New Mexico, which lived in the
cliffs, or, as the story came to him, in high houses
of clay and stone, having door-posts lined with
emeralds, he offered to equip a force at his own
expense to win a new empire for Spain.   He was
appointed governor to Cuba with oversight also
of Florida, which meant all the land north of the
Gulf of Mexico, extending indefinitely northward
and westward.

Having the right of exploration, the young soldier
called together a company of adventurous spirits
and equipped them handsomely.   In May, 1539, he
landed at Tampa Bay with nearly nine hundred

men mostly in the prime of youth, in gayest dress and armor. They were furnished with playing-cards for games, priests and altars for religion, horses for the officers and cavalry, and a large drove of hogs for fresh food. It was as gay, as fanatical, as wicked a company as ever set foot on any shore. They came with mixed motives, to kill, enslave, and conquer in the name of God. They had bloodhounds and manacles for the natives, whom they intended to catch. They were as zealous as they were avaricious, confidently expecting to win, as Pizarro and Cortez had done, a new empire, rich in gold.

Under splendid banners and crosses, which he had erected, and with dazzling ceremonies, de Soto consecrated the land to God and the King. It was now to be seen whether the man who had succeeded so grandly in the South American highlands could subdue the wilderness of a flat region, full of mud and malaria, and totally different in all its aspects from the mountains and forests of the southern continent.

The march northward and westward was begun amid swamps and thickets. The hostile natives, the malarious climate, the new and strange diseases, and the constant danger of hunger was terrible, but to the end of his life, de Soto's men kept discipline and obeyed him.

During their hunt for gold and for Indian treasure-cities, they met with many wonders. Two escaped Spanish captives joined them. They put the Indian slaves whom they kidnapped, in iron collars and chains, and made them grind corn and carry packs. In October the harbor of Pensacola was discovered, and word was sent to Cuba for supplies to be forwarded next year. Turning to the northeast, they crossed during March and April the rich plains and rivers of Georgia, passing through a region populated by the ancestors of the now civilized tribes in the Indian Territory. In May they entered the Cherokee country. Fearing to cross the mountains, they wandered about in Alabama, reaching the large Indian town of Mobile near the middle of October. Here a great battle ensued, for the Indians, refusing to let these slave-makers occupy their houses, fought with splendid courage. Only after a desperate conflict and repeated cavalry charges, did the white warriors with armor and sword, guns and horses, win costly victory over the men of the stone age. Of the Spanish horses, twelve were killed and seventy injured; of the men, eighteen were slain and one hundred and fifty had arrow wounds. In the burning town the Spaniards lost their baggage and trophies. Twenty-five hundred of the natives, it is recorded, were killed, burned, or suffocated.

Only five hundred tattered men in rusty armor

now remained of the original nine hundred. Marching north through the Chickasaw country, they seized
the wigwams and corn of the Indians and spent the
winter on the Yazoo River. In the spring, rather
than furnish two hundred slaves to de Soto, the
Indians set fire to the town, burning up many
horses, hogs, and "Christians," besides clothing and
weapons. The invaders expected now to be over-
whelmed in an attack by great numbers, but the
spirit of the half-naked whites rose to the emer-
gency. The Spaniards were good blacksmiths and
metal-workers. Within a week, at their forges, they
had made new weapons or mended old ones, and
were too well prepared to be safely meddled with by
men having only clubs and stone-headed arrows.
De Soto would not give up or turn back. Resum-
ing the march, after a week's toiling through swamp
and forest, they reached the muddy Mississippi, near
what is now Memphis.

The fear of men who wore steel hats and fought
on horses, had preceded them, and a fleet of two
hundred canoes filled with Indians, their chief in
feathers and state dress, came down the river to
offer presents of food, fish, and persimmon bread.
The horses could not be got across the mile-wide
river in bark canoes, which they would have
swamped or kicked through, so the Spaniards had
to build barges.

How strange it seems that two Spanish expeditions, each chasing the phantom of " the Seven Cities
rich in gold," — an idea which they had in their
brains before leaving Europe, — were within a few
leagues of each other at this time, and were mutually ignorant of each other's presence. In midsummer, 1541, Coronado, who from Mexico had
traversed Arizona and New Mexico, and who, having found that " the Seven Cities of Cibola " were
only Indian villages with no gold, was seeking other
gleaming phantoms among buffaloes and savages in
central Kansas; while at the same time de Soto,
on a similar hunt, was chasing brain spectres and
piercing himself with many sorrows. They never
met on earth to compare experiences, although both
were in Arkansas.

De Soto's party moved north into Missouri and
up along the banks of the Father of Rivers. The
Indians believed the white men to be gods who
were able to heal the blind. The explorers enjoyed
the bountiful crop of nuts, berries, and fruits of the
land. At the northernmost point of their travels
they spent a month, hearing of bisons, but not of
any gold. Then they marched westward, spending
the winter along the line of the Washita River, mur-
dering, burning, mutilating, or enslaving the savages,
as suited their whim, making a hell on earth in their
rage and disappointment.

Discouraged and melancholy, de Soto now again turned towards the Mississippi, where the tattered remnants of his host gathered round him, as he named his successor, May 20, 1542. The next day he breathed his last. Some priests were yet left in the company, and requiem mass was celebrated over his body. At midnight the corpse, wrapped up and weighted to sink, was dropped into the river. So perished the discoverer of the Mississippi, but it was very long before his widow in Cuba, whom he had left as a bride, heard of his melancholy end. Both Coronado and de Soto left home, wife, comforts, and fortune to hunt ghosts.

Still in the hope of reaching wealth, and too proud to give up and return home poor, the survivors wandered on westward toward Mexico and to the buffalo pastures and hunting-grounds of the Pawnees and Comanches; but, in despair, they again turned to the great river in December. Five months were spent in building seven undecked boats. Nails were made out of the chains and collars used on the Indian slaves. Hogs, horses, and game were killed and their flesh dried, the corn stores of the Indians were robbed, and barrels to hold fresh water were made. Then, with the rising flood they started down the river on their fresh and salt water journey to Mexico. In seventeen days they had reached the Gulf. In about forty days more the three hundred and nineteen survivors arrived at Panuca in Mexico, thus ending five years of suffering and of the infliction of suffering on others.

This was the first inland navigation of American waters by Europeans. De Soto's men had probably traversed the territory of no fewer than eleven or twelve of the states of our union, from Florida to Texas.

CHAPTER XVI.

IT is time now to tell of Cabeza de Vaca's most
wonderful overland travels from Tampa Bay
to the City of Mexico, and how his explorations prepared the way for the Spanish settlements and colonies in Texas, New Mexico, Arizona, and California.
Let us glance at his early history and see what kind
of a man he was, and what strange vicissitudes he
underwent. His full name was Alvar Nuñez Cabeza
de Vaca. His ancestors had won their family name
two centuries before, in battle against the Moors.
His grandfather had conquered the Canary Islands
for the King of Spain. These islands, long before
the time of Columbus and until the days of
Raleigh's Virginia colonies, formed the far western
limit of the old world. From the Canaries, which
are still famous for their wines and song birds,
most of the early exploring expeditions southward
and westward sailed.

At the Isle of Misfortune, as we remember,
Cabeza de Vaca had been left behind, because too
ill to walk, but he held on to life. As warm

M

weather advanced, he recovered and actually won his way to the confidence of the Indians. After winning success as a pedestrian, merchant, and doctor among the natives, he at last reached Mexico and afterwards returned to his European home. He came back to America as Governor of Paraguay; he failed and returned to Spain as a convict. He was kept in prison eight years, and when released lived at Seville until 1564.

In 1542 Cabeza de Vaca produced the book which gives us the first written account of the southern part of our great country. In this, he tells us, not only about himself, but also about the Indians. He describes their modes of life in war and peace, and their commerce. It was this devout Catholic who first taught the southern Indians the truths of the Christian religion. He was really the first missionary among them and learned their language. From him, the ancestors of the Cherokees, Choctaws, Chickasaws, and other civilized tribes learned about God and Christ and creation, and received an outline of the Bible story. He laid the foundations on which in later times other missionaries builded. He thus prepared the way for their success. From Cabeza de Vaca to the Cherokee Bible, and the Cherokee Indians of to-day, it is a long story of wrongs and sorrows, but also of progress.

How this Spaniard became a doctor and a merchant is told in his own book. Even when he was on Misfortune Island the Indians wished to make the white men physicians, but the proposition was received with hearty laughter. The Spaniards took the matter as a joke and thought the Indians were making fun of them, but the redskins were so much in earnest that they kept the white men hungry until they should yield and be obedient. The Indian theory was, that it was not necessary to know anything especially about roots or herbs, pills or tonics, but that as the sticks and stones and birds and beasts and reptiles had healing power, such strange creatures as white men must certainly be able to drive away diseases.

Many of these Indians were very poor and miserable, having little to eat. Their life consisted chiefly in wandering from one place of food to another. As their white slave was too weak to draw a bow, to follow and trap animals, or to carry wood and water, even if they had allowed him to do that which was squaw's work, they let him wander about to find his own food, and go and come as he chose. Gradually, as his strength returned, he made long journeys up and down the coast. Soon he began to trade, acting as importer and exporter. He brought sea-snails, corn, medicine, shells, sea-beads, and other things from among the coast

Indians and traded off his wares among the interior
tribes for skins, red ochre, flints for arrow-heads,
cement, reeds for arrow-shafts, and red-dyed tassels
of deerskin. Everywhere the Indians treated him
kindly and gave him food for his wares. As in the
time of war the Indians of mutually hostile tribes
could not themselves traffic, they were only too glad
to have this neutral peddler carry on the business of
a common carrier, which he did to his own profit.
He was not only the first commercial traveller in
North America, but was also the first white man
who ever saw or heard of the bison or buffalo, and
the first to describe what he called the "hunch-back
cows."

Gradually he learned from the medicine men the
tricks of their profession. All over the world, savages, who know nothing of the real causes and nature
of disease, think that sickness and death come from
spells or witchcraft caused by some enemy, or by
being possessed of demons. Hence, the "medicine
men" or wizards pretend by devilish tricks, noises,
or by making themselves hideous, to frighten and
drive out the imp or to neutralize the spell. Soon
this lonely Spaniard had a great reputation as one
who could suck out the poison, the imaginary stone
or the thorn which made the trouble, for the mind-
cure existed then as now. Instead of surgical instruments and pill-boxes, his chief aid in influencing

patients was a rattle made of a dried bladder skin
with beans inside.

Once on a long journey, after having occasionally
heard rumors of the presence of his countrymen, he
wandered into Texas. There he found two Spaniards and a negro named Stephen, or Estevanico,
and these four, naked and hungry, resolved to set
out for Mexico. In August, 1535, they reached a
tribe where each of the four practised medicine, so
they quickly became men of renown and importance.
They crossed Texas and went through the modern Mexican provinces of Chihuahua and Sonora.
Everywhere they stopped to heal the sick. Not content with what they had learned from the Indians,
they earnestly prayed to God for their patients. It
is more than probable that after their departure
these four strangers were themselves made into gods
and their memory worshipped. At least, we may
infer as much from what we know has happened in
old Japan again and again. Indeed, pretty much
the whole stock of heathen gods are only men with
posthumous reputation for power.

The travellers were agreeably surprised to find
fields in which beans and pumpkins were cultivated,
and that their red owners lived in houses made of
timber and sod, like our "sod-shacks" in the new
territories. The women were decently dressed in
cotton clothing, and even washed their clothes, using

soap-root, which is still employed by our own Indians and Mexicans. It was like a royal feast when they had cooked deer's hearts to eat during their three days' stay in one town. Then they met an Indian having on his necklace a horseshoe nail and the buckle of a sword belt, which he said he had got from men with beards who had come from the sky and fought his people. This was their first sight in eight years of anything European.

In Sinaloa, they heard of Spanish slave-catchers who had just left the place. After a hurried march, they overtook on the next day four Spaniards, to whom, though nearly overcome with emotion, they told their story, which seemed incredible. The Spanish officers were not very hospitable to these sun-burned, savage-looking men of matted hair and tangled beard, who talked so excitedly, and the four survivors were abused in various ways; but finally, May 1, 1536, they reached Culiacan, and later the City of Mexico. They had now to train themselves to be white men in habits, and to eat the food and wear the clothes of civilization.

In August, 1537, after a walk of probably over ten thousand miles, and having been the means of stimulating expeditions which opened Arizona and New Mexico to Spanish civilization, and our Indian Territory, Kansas, and Colorado to exploration, Cabeza de Vaca reached Spain. It was his accounts

of the countries he had traversed, and his reports of
" the Seven Cities of Cibola, full of gold " of which
he had heard, but had not seen, that started both
Coronado and de Soto, the one from the east, and
the other from the west, on their terrible marches.
It was a double chase after the shadows of a fairy
tale.

CHAPTER XVII.

ONE name that ought never to be forgotten by Americans is that of Brother Mark, or Fray Marcus, who heard of the Seven Cities of Cibola from Cabeza de Vaca on his arrival in Mexico, and at once resolved to visit them. Brother Mark was another of that noble Italian band who, besides Cabot and Columbus, did so much to make America known. He was born in that city of Nice, over which, in 1860, the soldier Garibaldi's heart was nearly broken, because Count Cavour the statesman ceded it to France. Mark had come to America with Pizarro in 1531. After his experiences in Peru he was in Guatemala and then came to Mexico.

Ordered by his superior, not to needlessly expose his life to danger, he, in the spring of 1539, started with the black man Estevanico and a few Indians to walk the whole distance from the City of Mexico to Zuñi land. Following the coast of the Southern Sea, as the Spaniards called the Pacific Ocean, until near Matape, he ordered the negro forward. He told him to send back reports by Indian messengers, by means of large or small crosses on pieces of white wood, enlarging the marks according as the news was encouraging.

Carrying his medicine rattle and making use of his powers as a wizard, this " Black Mexican," as the Zuñi Indians still call him, made a wonderful impression and great progress, and finally reached the Zuñi pueblos or towns. There he seems to have abused his privileges, by behaving rudely to the men and insulting the women, and was killed. Perhaps this was the first blood of an African negro shed on what is now United States soil.

Brother Mark received very good tidings in the form of large cross-marks on white wood, until he got within sight of the Zuñi villages, where some hungry and tattered companions of black Stephen met him and told him the bad news. Mounting a hill from which he could overlook the promised land, Mark saw large houses several stories high in what seemed a city full of people dressed in cotton. He planted a cross on this prospect hill and then made a hasty retreat.

Brother Mark saved his head by using his heels, as he had been ordered to do. Getting back into Mexico, he told so wonderful a story that he was considered the biggest liar Spain had thus far produced. Like Mendez Pinto, who, when he talked

of Japan, was set down as *mendacious*, and Marco
Polo, who was called " Millioner " or exaggerator, so
the good brother was at first quoted as an edifying
but highly untrustworthy story-teller. In reality,
his written report, as read to-day and confirmed by
historical research, is wonderfully accurate. He
said nothing of gold, but all Spaniards then imagined that where population and fertile soil existed,
there must be gold in plenty.

An expedition, quickly fitted out and with
Brother Mark serving as land pilot, started for
Zuñi. There they arrived in due time, but the
friar had to leave the party on account of rheuma-
tism. He came back to live in the City of Mexico,
until 1558, when he died. Brother Mark was the
discoverer of New Mexico.

The exploring expedition by which New Mexico
was made known, was commanded by Francisco
Vasquez de Coronado, a governor of the Mexican
province of New Galicia. He was a city-bred man,
knowing little of frontier life, but was full of the
idea of finding on land the " Seven Cities rich in
gold," which John Cabot had tried to discover in the
ocean. Coronado left behind him wife and home,
fortune and comforts. At his own expense, he had
equipped this expedition of three hundred Spaniards and eight hundred Indians, with a thousand
spare or pack horses, many sheep and swine, and

six small cannon, which cost him what would now be nearly a quarter of a million dollars, and he left home deeply in debt.

It has been said that one reason why this band of new explorers had been so promptly raised and sent off, was because it was thought that they were leaving their country for their country's good. The little army was composed chiefly of young Spaniards who were too fond of drawing their swords and of engaging in other activities not popular in a settled community. They were not only sent away; they were ordered not to come back, but remain as colonists.

To shorten a long story, with a fleet by sea and a little army by land to aid him, Coronado and a picked guard of fifty horsemen went ahead quickly and reached Zuñi land early in July. Capturing the Indian town without difficulty, he sent parties to seize the villages of cliff-dwellers at Moqui, to the grand cañon of Colorado, and to the Pueblo in northern New Mexico. Yet he found nothing that corresponded to the fairy tales he had heard or thought he heard.

During the winter Coronado, now reinforced, marched to the Rio Grande, among the Pecos tribes, where he heard of the Quivira, which he understood was a large city, full of pure gold. The man who, by signs, told him this story, was a captive Indian

from the region of the buffaloes in Kansas. He
had been taken prisoner by the Pecos when on a
hunt and wanted to get back home. The Spaniards called him "the Turk," thinking he looked
like one.

Again lured by a new golden myth, Coronado
and his men tramped across Texas, surviving awful
dangers and hardships, and reaching far into the
Indian Territory. On the great prairies, seeing
nothing but the sky and buffaloes, they wandered
round and round in a circle, losing their way.
They ruthlessly slaughtered bulls and cows by the
hundreds. They found only savages dressed in
leather clothes and living in tents.

By this time, believing himself to have been
deceived, Coronado selected thirty men to go forward with him while the main body marched southward to the Rio Grande. He did not get to the
Mississippi River, where he might have met de Soto
and his band, and found his countrymen in like
quest and plight with himself. With his thirty
men, he went northward into Kansas and possibly
Nebraska; but, though he met the Quivira Indians,
he found them to be only buffalo-hunters living on
the plains, and knowing nothing of the yellow metal.

They first put "the Turk" in chains and then
hanged him. It is very doubtful whether, until he
saw the Spaniards, this savage knew what gold was.

During Coronado's absence in the northward, the other Spaniards, who had been left waiting, amused themselves by slaughtering the bisons, both bulls and cows, littering the plains with over five hundred carcasses. Many of these "hunch-backed" oxen were fierce and showed fight, killing several horses. The Spaniards enjoyed the sport as if they had been at home, where bull fights are still common. They thus began the extinction of that herd of over five millions of beef-producing bisons; which, in the northern pasture, was exterminated between the years of 1871 and 1875, the southern portion being finally destroyed between 1881 and 1883. The cow-boy and domestic cattle have, in this region, taken the place of Spaniard, Indian, and bison.

So, after all, unable to found a colony, and poor and empty, Coronado and his men came home with no golden fleece, and shorn of nearly everything but life itself. Unwelcomed and undesired, Coronado and about one hundred followers reached the City of Mexico in midsummer, 1542.

In our minds we usually associate the Spanish-American explorer with a horse, the animal which he introduced into the new world. Yet the Spaniard was more than a cavalier or centaur. Most of his greatest land explorations were made on foot. In bands and companies these searchers for gold,

danger, and fame, overran not only the South
American continent, but also Mexico, the whole region of the present Cotton States, Texas, and the
country west and southwest of Kansas and Colorado.
Where there were no paths and often no water,
grim and determined men in chase of phantoms,
and missionaries eager to save souls, tramped. If
Cabeza de Vaca walked his thousands, his country-
man, Andres del Campo, walked his tens of thousands. The former, a refugee with his face and
hope ever homeward, wrote a book and told his
story. Between April, 1542, and 1550, Andres
del Campo walked nearly nine years. He wrote
no book, but he explored Colorado and Kansas,
besides wandering to and fro in the great arid
regions between these American states and Mexico.
We shall see how it came about.

The missionary zeal of the friars, and their love
of souls, were even greater than the layman's love
of gold. In the autumn of 1542, Brother Padilla
led a little band into the newly explored regions.
The company consisted of some Indian boys, two
young men of Mexico named Lucas and Sebastian,
and the soldier Andres del Campo, who was on
horse, the others being on foot. They travelled
over the dry lands, across Colorado and through
Kansas, until they saw a cross which had been set
up by Coronado in one of the Sioux Indian towns.

BROTHER PADILLA FINDS THE CROSS SET UP BY CORONADO.

After laboring among the red men awhile, the friar decided to move to another tribe. On the first day's march out, some hostile savages in their war paint met them. The boys and horseman escaped, being urged by Brother Padilla to do so. The Indian archers made of the missionary a willing martyr, a St. Sebastian. He was shot to death with arrows, according to the fashion of savages, who empty their quivers where one shaft would suffice.

The full story of Andres del Campo and the young men Lucas and Sebastian, we do not know, except that they were captured by the Indians, made slaves, half-starved, and brutally treated. Yet, after eight years' wandering over the country from Kansas to Mexico, the three walked into Tampico, in 1550.

It looked now as though New Spain, as Mexico was then called, would not be greatly enlarged, if at all, during the sixteenth century, while all idea of a permanent colony was for the time being abandoned. Nevertheless, as Spaniards do not readily yield, they did not give up hope. Furthermore, it is not easy to dislodge the spectres of the brain. They brought to America from Europe old-world myths that are not yet utterly dead, and were then very much believed.

We must not forget that one of Coronado's parties went by water. Hernando Alarcon sailed along the Pacific coast and up the Gulf of Old California. Unable to force his ships against the current of the Colorado River, he went up in two boats a distance of eighty leagues, finding houses and inhabitants. Very probably he reached a point as far north as the great bend where it turns off to the right and east, at the foot of a mountain range. There he heard of the death of a negro and the capture of the Zuñi villages by the Spaniards. He thought it best not to undertake the land journey eastward, and so he returned to Mexico. He thus explored the Vermilion or Red Sea, as the Gulf of Old California was then called, and looked upon the soil of three of our United States, — California, Nevada, and Arizona.

Thus inland California was seen on its western side from a river boat. Its seacoast was explored from the Pacific, three years later, by Juan Rodrigues Cabrillo, a Portuguese in the Spanish service, who named Cape Mendoza, now Cape Mendocino, and the Farallone Islands. In 1592, a Spanish navigator sailed as far north as British America, entering and naming the strait of Juan de Fuca, which forms our national boundary between Vancouver's Island and Washington, — between British, and composite, or distinctive America.

California was reëxplored by the Spaniard Viscano in 1602, but was not colonized until the Franciscan fathers began their mission at San Diego in 1769. San Francisco, which has become the greatest city on the Pacific coast, was established in 1776, the year of our Independence, as the mission Dolores. By the middle of the sixteenth century, the Spaniards were acquainted with the two Americas as one continent. From the Chesapeake Bay, discovered by Spanish navigators and named the Bay of Santa Maria, to the fortieth degree of latitude on the western coast, they know North America in outline. Thus far all attempts to get a foothold within the present waters of the United States had resulted in dismal failures for the Spaniards. Yet while there was still comparative peace in Europe, before the Dutch and English heretics had begun to make trouble for the lord of half the world, and there were plenty of young Spaniards who wanted adventure and more money, and were ready to seek both at whatever cost, and while the missionary spirit was still strong, it looked as if North America, like South America, might yet become New Spain.

In 1560 Aviles de Menendez went to Florida, to establish there a little colony. He found a few French Huguenots on the ground, and these he promptly seized and hanged, "not as Frenchmen, but as heretics." He then built the town which he named after that greatest of all the African saints, the

N

mightiest of the church fathers who, among both
Protestant and Catholic theologians, is still so great
a favorite; for both the ultra-Montane Catholics and
the rigid Calvinists honor his memory and imitate
him in mind and ways.

The city of St. Augustine bade fair to be a new
Eternal City. Like the old saint's "City of God,"
it could not be destroyed. Though in 1560 the
French nobleman de Gourges captured its three
forts and hanged the colonists "not as Spaniards,
but as villains," and although in 1586 the Englishman Sir Francis Drake destroyed the colony,—
even as a dragon is supposed to swallow up the
moon,—yet St. Augustine was at once defiantly re-
built. It remained Spanish until 1763.

When it became English, Florida was explored
and described by the Dutchman Romaine, who
afterwards entered the service of Congress, became
an officer in the American army, built forts at West
Point, wrote one good book on Florida, and another
— the first ever printed in Hartford — justifying
the American independence of Great Britain, and
citing the example of the Dutch in revolting against
Spain in 1667. The Spaniards introduced the
orange into Florida, and the old stocks left by
them have been, by grafting, made to produce those
wonderful fruits — nature's bottles of wine — which
excel all others in the world. Except, however, a

few remnants of architecture and names of places, the Spanish mark upon Florida has been slight indeed.

By 1581, the year in which the United States of Netherland published their Declaration of Independence to Spain, the ill-fortune of Coronado had faded from most minds. A new generation had grown up. Men, then nearly forty years of age, had been born since he had reëntered Mexico with his tattered tramps. So again, some lion-hearted missionaries started on foot to reach Zuñi. Tarrying to preach the Gospel, they were slain by the Indians. Only nine soldiers, their companions, succeeded in reëxploring the country as far as Zuñi.

Next year, further addition was made to geography by Antonio Edpejo, a rich Cordovan, who started with fourteen men into the desert. He marched up along the Rio Grande, and passed the site of Albuquerque, a town taking its name after one in Spain, but suggesting also the name of the famous Portuguese conqueror of Malacca and first European navigator of the entire Red Sea. He met with little or no opposition from the Indians. He then turned westward and explored the northern parts of Arizona, visiting at least five of the cities of the "Cliff Brothers," or the Pueblo Indians. Returning again to the Rio Grande River and the

Pecos Indians, he went down the stream named after them, into Texas, and thence got back to Santa Barbara. He expected to return the next year and colonize New Mexico. However, he died soon afterward, and left a noble record of exploration, but established no colony.

Another who followed him, in 1590, was Gasper Casteno de Sousa. But having violated the requirements of the royal governor, he was arrested and brought home a prisoner.

The real colonizer of New Mexico was Juan de Onate, who founded the second oldest town in the United States, San Gabriel of the Spaniards, and also Santa Fé. Unlike Coronado and others who attempted to tame the wild and treeless wilderness, and to make the desert blossom as the rose, Onate was a native American frontiersman. Born in Mexico, he was thoroughly familiar with its mountains and deserts. He knew how to fight Indians, to find food and water, and to be patient and hopeful amid discouragements. His parents had come from the old country, and his father had discovered the silver mines of Zacatecas, then the richest in the world. Yet, so far from being satisfied with mining silver, Onate wanted to win new lands for Spain. The government would not provide funds for any more expeditions. After so many costly failures, the country north of Mexico was then regarded very much as most persons still look upon the Arctic regions, as a land in which there is nothing but disappointment and death.

With such a menace of starvation and poverty, after having lost so many men and so much money, — especially while so many thousand Spanish soldiers and so many ship-loads of Peruvian and Mexican silver were required to fight the little Dutch Republic, — the crown of Spain had early refused to send another man or to spend a fresh maravedi. So at great expense, Onate fitted out his own expedition. After many delays, and a refusal by the new viceroy even of permission to start, Onate set out in 1597. He had two hundred soldiers and as many colonists, among whom were women and children, besides tools and seed, sheep and cattle. Just north of where Santa Fé now stands he founded, in September, 1597, the town of St. Gabriel of the Spaniards.

Not satisfied with this, after seeing his colonists well under way in their new life, he explored the country round about and far northward, and in 1600 he reached Nebraska. Four years later he took thirty men and marched entirely across New Mexico and Arizona to the Gulf of California, returning safely to his colony in 1605, when he founded the city of the Holy Faith, or Santa Fé. The next year he again explored the regions to the northeast; but of these, his last movements, we know very little, if anything. In 1608 he retired from the government of the new province.

Thus, before a single English settlement had been successfully made in America, the whole of the southern part of the United States had been more or less explored by the Spaniards, who had also founded three cities.

CHAPTER XVIII.

RELIGION has always had much to do with geography and exploration. Pilgrims to sacred shrines in far countries, whether the Chinese to India, the Hindoos to Arabia, or the Europeans to Palestine, have added first and most to knowledge of strange lands. In the sixteenth century, until the Dutchmen taught a contrary lesson, the religion of a country was regulated by the King. "Who owns the region, owns the religion," was a maxim. Under the system of the Pope and the Emperor, when the Church and the Empire governed all Europe, for a nation to change its religion meant war. People had not then learned toleration or freedom of conscience.

The people of southern Europe had a curious idea in regard to the Reformation, for they thought it meant piracy. The first notion that many Spaniards and Italians had of a Protestant, was that he was a pirate. This was because as soon as the nations of northern Europe — French, Dutch, and English — began to reform their faith and worship,

they and the Spaniards and Portuguese became enemies and immediately sailed out on the seas to
capture each other's ships.   For a long while there
lingered in Spain and Italy this strange idea, that
the Dutch and English had become Protestants
simply because they could make themselves rich by
robbing Spanish commerce.   It was also believed
that the only motive which brought the Protestant
people to America was to secure Spanish gold and
treasure.   In this the Latin nations were not quite
right, though the English and Dutch desire to
defend themselves against the Spanish Giant Grim,
who claimed half the world and kept the Inquisition
ready to torture and burn all heretics, was a powerful motive in colonizing America.

Earlier than the discovery of America, and before
Spanish commerce had been greatly developed, the
Inquisition had been established in Spain, where
Church and State were one.   This Inquisition put
to death a great number of Jews and Moors.   Isabella, who aided Columbus, was one of the greatest
upholders of the horrible system.   Myriads of people
were tortured in the most barbarous way, and tens of
thousands more were burned to death.   After all the
Jews and Moors had been either incarcerated, incin-
erated, exiled, or forced to say that they were Christians, then the Inquisition was ready for new kinds
of heretics.   These were found plentifully among

those who liked to read the Bible in their own language and who had no use for Italian priests. Not content with haling Frenchmen, Spaniards, and Italians before the tribunals, the Spanish Inquisition caught the English sailors found in Spain and imprisoned, tortured, and burned them.

This made the English people hate the Inquisition and determine to do Spain all the harm they could. Unable to accomplish very much on land, they resolved to damage the Spaniards on the seas. They learned how to build swifter ships, that would spread more sail, and move forward whether the wind was in the wake or in their teeth, answering quickly to the helm. They made heavier and longer-ranged cannon. Pretty soon privateering became the rage. Men left commerce and the fisheries to make money in this lively, exciting, and lucrative business.

The English Jack did not care to declare war outright against the Spanish giant. England was too poor and weak to openly defy the owner of America, and as yet it seemed still uncertain whether the little Protestant states would be able to hold their own. On the other hand, Spain had her hands full in trying to colonize a new continent and to put down the revolt in the Netherlands. Until he could crush the Dutch United States, Philip II. did not care to venture upon open war with Elizabeth.

Consequently, during two generations there was a tremendous amount of bloodshed and murder, piracy and burning of ships and towns on both sides. There were all the horrors and wickedness of war, without its honorable and redeeming features.

Even the great Spanish Armada, which hoped to invade England and conquer it, was built and was sent in times of professed peace and without any declaration of war. This was the supreme effort of southern or papal Europe to put down the rights of conscience and freedom of thought in northern Europe. It was but one of several gigantic attempts which were made by the Latin nations and civilization to crush the Teutonic spirit and overwhelm the Germanic nations. Whether in the case of Arminius and Varus in the ancient forests of Teutoberg; at the Reformation; in the Dutch war of Independence; in the defeat of the Spanish Armada; in the Thirty Years War in Europe; in the two centuries of struggle between the French and English for possession of the North American continent; or in the attempt of foreigners to make the United States a country ruled by priests and soldiers, — the result was and will be ever the same. The Latin idea of the centralization of power over conscience and personal liberty will not work in America.

It was the west country of England that for the

most part, in the sixteenth century, produced deep-sea sailors and adventurous mariners and explorers. Those on the eastern and southeastern coast were chiefly petty traders, who rarely went out of sight of land. They trafficked in the North and Baltic seas and along the English Channel, but rarely sailed long out of sight of land.

In the western counties, Bristol had sent John Cabot. Devon produced many men of the sea. Plymouth was the centre of vast enterprise. The size of the ships in those days was very small. They were more like our little coasting-vessels, yachts, or sail-boats. Anything with a hull as big as one of our ordinary Erie Canal boats would have been a wonder, in the age of King Henry VIII. Yet, whereas our canal boats, when loaded, rise very little above the water, the sixteenth century ships had great castles built above their decks from the middle to the stern. Often there was a tower or "forecastle," as the name still is, near the bow. The heavy wooden turrets of some of the old fighting ships looked much like those of steel on our modern battle ships.

The opening of the Atlantic by the Spaniards revolutionized English seamanship and navigation, for long voyages required longer and larger ships. Henry VIII. first saw the importance of gunpowder in war, and imported Italians to cast new styles

of heavier artillery, but the first English ships that
came to America were armed with bows and arrows
rather than with cannon and round shot.

Columbus had offered the new world to Henry
VIII. when he sent his brother with maps and
globes, together with quotations from Plato and
Aristotle, to prove that there was a pathway to
China by sailing towards the setting sun; but
Henry could see no money in the venture, and
thought the idea a wild dream. So America was
found by the Spaniards and not by the English,
and little thought came to Englishmen of colonizing America.

Something unexpected happened in England to
turn the prows of her sailors across the Atlantic.
This was the divorce, by Henry VIII., of his Spanish wife, Catherine of Aragon, which made Henry
the public enemy of papal Europe. The divorce
seemed an insult to the Pope and to all people and
nations that looked on this Italian prince as the
vicar of God. Catherine was the daughter of Ferdinand and Isabella, the friends of Columbus. If
the mother, by sending the Genoese, had started
Spanish colonization in trans-Atlantic regions, the
daughter was the indirect means of despatching
Englishmen to America. She had already married
the oldest son of Henry VII. of England. In 1509,
under an express dispensation of the Pope, she

became the wife of Henry VIII., who was six years younger than herself. Her only living child became Queen Mary, who married Philip II., and was such a persecutor that she was called Bloody Mary. Some of the best churches now on English soil are built on the old ash-heaps where her victims were burnt.

Henry began to love Anna Boleyn. and wanted the Pope to divorce him from his Spanish Kate. The Pope declining, Henry divorced himself. In those days kings were a good deal more important than they are now. The people of northern Europe, and especially King Henry's countrymen, took up the quarrel and sided with him. At the Court of Rome, the focus of politics as well as religion, the English influence was foiled by the priests and lawyers from the land of the Bull-fight and the Inquisition, and Henry was excommunicated, but for this he cared not a fig. "Bluff King Hal" had just the spirit and habits which his countrymen admire. He was a fighter and could defend himself.

At once the English people became partisans for or against their king, and the modern political parties, the one the National, Liberal or Reforming, and the other, the Conservative or Catholic party, began their history. Henry, being intensely English, was very popular. When the Inquisition began to make more racks and buy more wood in order to

burn alive King Henry's subjects, then English
sailors longed to take their revenge on the seas.
America was the treasure house of the King of
Spain, and they proposed to help themselves to his
possessions. A tremendous zeal for exploration
and discovery now broke out among sailors and
landsmen in the British Isles, but it was not in the
interests of science. Their object was the Spanish
gold and silver beyond sea.

One Thomas Stukely was a specimen explorer
of the long line made famous by Hawkins and
Drake. Having a pretext to settle an English colony in Florida, Stukely collected one hundred tall
soldiers and set out from Plymouth in a ship of four
hundred tons. When once out of harbor, Stukely
said to his men, "The sea is my Florida," and
started on a piratical expedition to loot the cargoes
of plate ships from America. To this day, "plate,"
the tell-tale name for old silver and table service in
England, points to the days when the chief source
of plate was *plata*, or Spanish silver, not mined out
of the ground, but found on the ocean. Stukely
made Ireland his sally-port and base of supplies.
Other privateers and corsairs chose the Scilly Isles
as their headquarters. "The pirates of Penzance"
in the sixteenth century figured not in a comic
opera, but in reality.

The man who opened for Englishmen the path

to the West Indies, and, first in our English tongue, described Florida, was William Hawkins, the father of two more famous freebooters in as many generations. He stuck to business and avoided politics. He saw that there was money in seizing and selling negroes. In 1530 he made a voyage to Guinea and opened that African slave trade which enriched England during three centuries. He sold his captured flesh and blood to the Portuguese in South America. On his second voyage, having crossed the Atlantic, he brought back a savage Brazilian chief, who was a great curiosity in England. Hawkins is known to have made three voyages to Guinea and Brazil. "Guinea gold" was by this time well known in Queen Elizabeth's realm.

Thus began our ancestors' interest in strange peoples. From the first, the English were great kidnappers. They stole many natives, of various colors of cuticle, in order to show them in the counties at home. This was both to stir up interest in exploration schemes and to make money. At that time Moors, negroes, or men of reddish skin were a great curiosity. Their stone hatchets, bows and arrows, canoes and ornaments, seemed as wonderful as if brought from another planet. Later on, the North American Indians attracted great crowds. The London or Plymouth of that day were very different from these cities in our century,

when people of all nations may be met on the
streets. Shakespeare, in " The Tempest," speaks of
" salvages and men of Indes " and of the " holiday
fools," who will lay out ten Dutch farthings even
" to see a dead Indian." Like father, like son.
Where William Hawkins stole tens, his son John
caught and sold thousands of negroes.

With the intention of outdoing his father, Hawkins the second left Plymouth in 1562 for the
Canary Islands. Sailing down to Sierra Leone,
he captured his first cargo of three hundred black
men and carried them over to the town founded by
Columbus, Hispaniola, which had already become
the chief slave market of the new world. There,
Hawkins sold his human cattle at a high profit.
In return he brought home pearls, sugar, ginger,
and the spices which our forefathers liked so much,
besides some hides which he sent to Spain, then
the greatest country in Europe for boots and shoes.
Cordovan leather was everywhere famous, and the
" cordwainer " of modern days is a cordovan out of
Spain, — a shoemaker.

On his second voyage Hawkins was not less of
a trader, but more of an explorer. He had four
ships and nearly two hundred men. They went
first to Guinea, and then crossed the ocean, the
holds of their ships packed tight with poor negroes.
On the way over, their ships got into a calm, and for

twenty-one days they could not move. The danger
of their provisions running out was great, but in
March they reached the Spanish slave markets and
began selling their human freight. Hawkins made
surveys of other islands in the West Indies, took
soundings, studied the currents, made charts, and
sailed along the coast of Florida, giving us the first
description in our own language of the land which
now forms our most southern state.

Hawkins tells us about tobacco. He says that
the Indians, when they travelled, had a kind of dry
herb which they put into an earthen cup at the end
of a cane. This they fired, sucking the smoke
through the cane. This satisfied their hunger and
helped them to go without meat or drink. Hawkins helped the Huguenot colonists whom he met
in Florida. He noticed that these Frenchmen,
from a country of vineyards, had already made
twenty hogsheads of wine from the grapes that
grew in that region, and that they had all got into
the habit of smoking tobacco.

Hawkins tells us many other things about Florida. Indeed, it is possible that, take it altogether,
we have in his sketch the best account of any one
of our Atlantic coast states, at so early a period of
their history. He noticed that the tribal or com-
munal houses were as big as English barns. These
were made of tree trunks and poles covered with

o

palmetto leaves. Inside, the fire kept burning all
night.

The country abounded in deer and game, fish
and birds, millet, corn, grapes, besides very much
sorrel.   Hawkins describes the favorite dish of
boiled corn meal, which the Yankees afterwards
called "hasty pudding"; the Englishmen in Pennsylvania, who had come from the middle counties
of England, "mush"; while the Dutch adopted the
Indian word "suppawn." Hawkins may have called
it "pap." He says, "It maketh good meal, beaten
and sodden with water and eateth like that where-
with we feed children." He noticed that the
Frenchmen made soup of it.

When John Hawkins arrived home in England
with gold, silver, pearls, and jewels, there was great
excitement throughout the kingdom. The Queen
honored and rewarded the successful slaver, taking dinner with him on board of his ship, and grant-
ing him a coat of arms, whereon was a black shield
with a golden lion walking over the waves. His
crest was the figure of half a Moor; that is, a bound
and captive slave with bands of gold on his arms
and gold rings in his ears. Later on, this pious
slave-robber added, by official permission, the pilgrim's scallop shell in gold, between the cross-staff
of a palmer or pilgrim to the Holy Land.

CHAPTER XIX.

THE Englishman's crusade of the sixteenth century was for slaves and money. Henceforth
to him America was " the land of the Almighty Dollar," — the latter term being even then in vogue for
a silver coin. Englishmen now became warmly
interested in the promising new world. They even
began to think a little of colonization, but much
more of the money to be gotten by trading negroes
and robbing the Spaniards.

Guinea gold flowed into the English mint,
though it was not till 1664 that the coin of that
name was struck. The coinage of the guinea lasted
till 1817. Since then a guinea is a sentimental
sum, but not a coin. A gift, an honorarium for a
speech, sermon, or lecture, or a polite present, is
made in guineas. Wages and bargains are made
in the pounds, shillings, and pence of the mediæval
Teutonic era still retained by British people.

In Spain, Philip II. got fearfully excited over the
idea of the English burglars, as he considered them,

breaking into his private treasure house. We soon
find him issuing edicts that no Englishman of any
creed or kind should be allowed in the West Indies. When edicts, as he found, were of no use, he
set up the Inquisition in Mexico to torture and
burn these foreigners from northern Europe, who
singed his beard, picked his pockets, and captured
his ships. While they did these things, he could
not pay his troops who were fighting to destroy the
Dutch United States. Hence, his mercenaries
mutinied, and the Netherlanders got the advantage
over him.

With such tokens of favor from his queen, such
rich profits in prospect, and withal, considering it
highly pious and proper to steal men, and sell them
for money, we find Hawkins starting out again in
1567. This time Francis Drake commanded the
Judith, while Hawkins himself was in his old ship,
the *Jesus*. The little hawk was the pioneer of the
dragon. Where Hawkins swooped on chickens
and picked bones, Drake was to swallow whole
towns and fleets.

Capturing five hundred negroes, though having
to feed them during seven weeks, they finally arrived
in the West Indies, where the people had been
warned against them. Nevertheless, as the Spanish
farmers and miners wanted slave labor, there was a
chance to sell, though the Englishmen sometimes

had to fight before getting permission to trade. Storm-beaten, they put into the harbor of Vera Cruz, near which is the famous castle San Juan d'Uloa, which was bombarded by our army and navy in 1846. A great Spanish fleet of twelve ships arriving, the English were attacked, and only the two little ships the *Minion* and the *Judith* reached England in January, 1669. The poor Englishmen captured were horribly tortured by the Inquisition.

Where Hawkins had been as Saul, Drake was now as David against the Spanish Philistines. He took terrible revenge for the "perfidy" of the Spaniards. Henceforth he devoted his life to doing as much injury to the King of Spain as possible. He did not pretend to be either an explorer or a trader; but only a private avenger against the Spaniards. Queen Elizabeth was only too glad to let him go forth on his own risk and account. This would save her the trouble of declaring war while hurting her enemies. She could approve or disown Drake as suited her policy. Drake made voyages to the West Indies in the years 1570, 1571, and 1572. Marching across the Isthmus, with the aid of the Maroons, a tribe of Indians reinforced with runaway black slaves, he climbed a tree, in the midst of the densely forested mountains. Seeing the great blue Pacific Ocean melting in the distance of silvery haze, he descended, fell on his knees, and prayed to God that some time he might sail on that sea and " make a perfect discovery of the same."

After further service in English waters on the Queen's behalf, Drake was ready in 1577 for another piratical raid on the Spaniards, which proved to be in the end " the first English furrow ploughed round the world." Of his ships, the *Pelican*, the *Elizabeth*, *Swan*, *Marigold*, and *Christopher*, the largest was of one hundred, and the smallest of fifteen tons. The *Pelican* had twenty cannon mounted on carriages, besides others in the hold. It was common in those days for guns, which could only fire stones and small balls, to burst, or be otherwise disabled. An extra lot was therefore taken in and stowed away in the hold to be used when wanted.

Some idea of Drake's love of luxury and the wealth he had gotten, may be learned when we read that besides having musicians and rich furniture, all the vessels on the table and even many in the cook room were of pure silver. In order to mislead the Spanish envoy at London, Drake pretended to be going to Egypt, but when once out of the English Channel his prows were turned to the southwest, to the lands of El Dorado, — of silver, gold, and gems, — South America.

Early in June they reached Port Saint Julian on the south coast of Patagonia, where they spent two months. One of the first sights they saw on arriv-

ing were the well-picked and whitened bones of a
human skeleton, at the base of a gibbet, on which
Magellan had hanged one of his mutineers. Drake,
no better or worse, at this same place, put to death
one of the men of his command whom he believed
to be treacherous. After the southern winter was
over, they sailed southward, meeting with driving
storms. They passed through the Straits of Magellan and got out into the Pacific, but alone. Drake's
ship was indeed like a pelican in the wilderness,
for none other of his squadron was in sight. The
other ships had foundered or been shipwrecked, or
the commanders had deserted this man whom the
Spaniards always called "the dragon." Drake
landed on a point of land and gave the name of
Elizabeth Island to Terra del Fuego, or the Land
of Fire. His tree-top glimpse had now become a
boundless vision.

Out into the Pacific he sailed northward, occasionally stopping for supplies. At Valparaiso he
robbed a Spanish ship, and then kept upward along
the coast, getting fresh water or provisions as he
needed them. At Arica he made a tremendous
haul, plundering the Spanish ships of their gold,
silver, jewels, and spices, not caring for anything
but what he could easily carry, for he had now but
one ship. Arica is a town of Chili, whence now
starts a railroad into the interior.

Callao was another rich place full of plunder, where Drake also got news from Europe. With a cart-load or more of silver in her gizzard, the *Pelican* now spread her white wings in pursuit of a treasure ship that had sailed two weeks before. Coming up with and capturing her on the first of March, Drake found her cargo to consist of about three million dollars' worth of bullion, coined and uncoined money, metallic vessels and gems; or, what would be equal in our time, to about twelve millions of dollars. There were thirteen boxes of the silver coin called real, which until lately was called in our country "levy" or "bit," the half being "fip." These words are the English contractions of eleven-penny and five-penny bits or pieces. Reals were also called "Spanish shillings," and the "piece of eight," or eight shillings, a dollar. This capture gave the Englishmen plenty of small change for further use.

There were also eighty pounds' weight of gold, twenty-six tons of uncoined silver, and an enormous golden cross with emeralds as large as pigeon eggs. Drake was kind enough not to put the Spaniards to death, though in those days of brutal war the captors on either side usually threw the captured overboard. After six days he gave the captain a change of linen and some provisions and let him and the crew go. He could afford to throw the shell away, after having opened the oyster and eaten the meat.

All this time wondering what had become of his other ships, Drake kept northward, in the path of the Spanish explorers who had been before him. Everything was new, wild, and wonderful to his men. Some things were pleasant and some things otherwise. On one island an earthquake gave them a new and terrifying sensation.

In 1510, thirty years before Drake was born, a Spaniard had written a novel telling about a fabulous island rich in gold and precious stones, — somewhat akin to Antilia, or the Japanese Horai. From this romance the name California received its name. Thirty-six years before Drake, Cabrillo had discovered the coast line of this, one of the most important states of the American Union, but when Drake saw California, it was inhabited only by savages of the stone age. Strangely enough, we know more about the exact discovery and exploration of our western or Pacific coast (with the names and dates, while the determinations of latitude and longitude are more full and exact) than of our eastern coast, which is nearest to Europe.

Drake no doubt at this time had the map of Furnala, made in 1574, which pictures Japan as if it were only a few miles off from the coast of North America. His men found it very cold even in

June and July, the ground without greenness, and
the natives wearing furs. The Pacific coast climate
has not changed very much in three centuries.
One Indian came out in a canoe and threw some
tobacco on board the ship. No doubt the man in
the canoe made an offering of tobacco, as an act of
worship, supposing that the men in the *Pelican*
were gods, for he would take nothing in exchange
except a hat which was thrown him. Drake tried
to find the western end of a passage homeward
into the Atlantic Ocean, but was disappointed. He
went no farther north than Oregon, which he named
New Albion, after his native country, because the
white cliffs which he saw reminded him of the
southern sea-face of his own land.

Giving up all idea of sailing eastward through
the continent of America, and in that way getting
back to England, Drake determined to return by
the way of the Philippines and the Cape of Good
Hope. He at once entrenched his camp and, setting up tents, began the work of refitting his ship.
An immense crowd of Indians came on the ground,
bringing feathers and tobacco as presents, the chief
making a long speech which tired the Englishmen to listen to, they not being able to understand a word. In return, Drake lifted up his eyes
to heaven and calling on his men to pray with him,
they all knelt down together. After prayer, they

sang songs, read chapters of the Bible, and returned presents to the Indians.

Other ceremonies followed a few days later, when the great war chief and his body-guard visited the English settlement. In their ceremonies, Drake understood them to mean that they wanted to become the subjects of the white man. They put one of the feather crowns upon Drake's head and hung one of their great chains made of bone upon his neck. So in the name and to the use of Queen Elizabeth, Drake took the sceptre, crown, and dignity of the country into his hands.

While his ship was being braced and cleansed, Drake travelled inland and saw enormous herds of deer, and what he thought were conies or rabbits, but were probably opossums. He erected a post on which he affixed a plate of brass, engraved with the Queen's name, with the date of landing, and the gift of the country by the people. He also gave specimens of the English sixpences to the people. Having driven fresh oakum between his planks, mended his cordage, strengthened his masts, and filled the water casks, Drake turned his prow westward. The friendly savages built fires on the hills and kept them up as long as the *Pelican* was in sight.

Drake sailed successfully round the Cape of Good Hope. On September 26, 1580, in grand

style, with gilded masts, and his sailors dressed in
silk, gold, and gems, he sailed into Plymouth. He
was the British Puck. He had put a girdle round the
earth. He then went to Court and told his adventures.

So far from the Queen or the government either
disowning Drake's acts as those of a pirate, or of
making any claim to land which Drake had discovered, no one ever thought of this as a voyage of
exploration at the time or until hundreds of years
afterwards. As usual, the Spanish envoy in London made protest against Drake's piracy, but Elizabeth was only too proud of the man, who, besides
circumnavigating the globe, could bring home such
a shipload of jewels, coin, and bullion. She made
Drake a knight, and ordered the ship *Pelican* to
be carefully kept. To-day in the Bodleian Library
at Oxford there is a chair made of her timber by
Sir John Davis, the Arctic navigator.

Very appropriately, three hundred years afterwards, Christian men in America erected a cross
on the Oregon coast to commemorate this visit of
Albion's great navigator and the first Englishman
who went round the globe.

Both Drake and Hawkins afterwards tried their
hand against the Spaniards of the West Indies, but
Hawkins died of a wound, and Drake of a fever, and
the expedition ended in loss and misery. There are
some Englishmen who still hope that the leaden

coffin in which Drake's body was sunk may be recovered and his bones yet find a resting-place in his
homeland. In "Westward Ho," the novel, Charles
Kingsley tells grandly the story of these west-
country freebooters.

Drake and Hawkins were among the first English
heroes of the sea. They set the example very often
since followed by pious pirates and industrious buccaneers. In diplomacy, war, statecraft, and religion,
England has never lacked men of action, unscrupu-
lous men whose sincere purpose — as sincere as that
of a Spanish heretic-burner — has been to make
England great. They set an example which Americans have too often followed. One of our naval
officers made it his motto, "Right or wrong, my
country," thus setting patriotism above righteousness, — a principle that makes of earth a hell.

From the time of Hawkins and Drake, and long
after, English sailors dressed in gay colors, wore
gold earrings in their ears, and were very fond of
flags and decorations. The brutalities of war and
ship life were very great then, and the barbarities in
the name of religion showed how little the teachings
and life of Jesus were understood. It took centuries for our fathers to learn that gain is not godliness,
that slave-catching is inhuman, and that to persecute
a man who differs from you in religion is not Christ-
like, but devilish.

Yet there were even in the sixteenth century, some moderate men in power, like the republican president of the Dutch United States, William the Silent, who preached and practised the toleration which is common to-day. In the countries where the Reformed churches were national or political, Bible-reading people nicknamed " Anabaptists" were already teaching the doctrines which are now settled in the Constitution of the United States and commonplace in our country. Both Protestants and Catholics, in every country except Holland, from Russia to England, persecuted and killed these non-political Christians. Some of these separatists, also, abused their liberty and became anarchists, but the Anabaptists, so-called, and the Mennonites are the real spiritual ancestors of most American Christians in many denominations.

CHAPTER XX.

THE English, during the time of the Tudors, became a new nation. The old Wars of the Roses, the long quarrels between the nobility, were over. A closer union between the throne and the people resulted. England began to do something else than to raise sheep and wool. King Henry had encouraged his subjects to trade in the Netherlands and had enlarged the British navy. Queen Elizabeth was just the kind of a woman to carry out her father's plans and even go beyond them. Henry was intensely English and, therefore, with all his faults he was very popular. His daughter was, like him, a strong character. Though fickle and vain, coquettish and fond of flattery, with a temper not always kept under control, she yet loved her country and people. She took good care of the finances and had great ability in governing. She encouraged her sailors and increased the loyalty of the people to the throne.

The days of chivalry were not yet over, but the English knights instead of going on crusades, now

went to fight the Spaniards, by helping the Dutch
republicans in their war of independence, by looting
the Spanish plate fleets from the West Indies, or by
attempting commerce or explorations.

One of the best dressed and handsomest of these
knights was Walter Raleigh, a Devonshire man born
in 1552. When a student at Oxford, he left his
books to go as volunteer on behalf of Huguenot liberty under Admiral Coligny. Afterwards he served
in the Dutch army under William of Orange. His
fight with Spain lasted during his whole life. His
supreme idea was to make England great. He as-
pired to clip the wings of Spain, which, like a great
eagle, rampant and eager to make Holland and England its prey, seemed to overshadow Europe. He
saw that the enemy had got rich by his possessions
in America, and he proposed to make England
mighty and opulent in the same way. When the
colony sent out to Florida by Coligny had been destroyed by the Spaniard Menendez, Raleigh, who was
a sailor as well as a soldier, wanted at once to settle
and develop North America. His first cruise westward was in 1578 in command of the ship *Falcon*
under Sir Humphrey Gilbert.

In those days it was very hard to provision a ship
for a long voyage. Little was then known about
preserving food in such quantity and variety so as
to keep off that horrible disease called the scurvy.

Many a voyage which began with promise ended in disaster because of the scurvy or of hunger. However brave in spirit, men cannot sail or work on empty stomachs. Even hearts of oak require plenty of stimulus. In our day the average ship is healthier than the average house, but it was not so then. All of Gilbert's ships had to turn back. Raleigh himself tried to reach the West Indies, but when near the Cape de Verde Islands his bread-bags were nearly empty, and he had to turn back. Fighting both the storms and the Spaniards on the way, he reached Plymouth, in May, 1579.

Exploration is very costly business. Some one must pay the bills. Raleigh made up his mind to get rich first and then to be his own banker. He entered the Queen's service in Ireland and was very successful. He was not only brave, but witty and learned. He dressed magnificently and knew just how to please the coquettish Queen Elizabeth. He succeeded in making a fortune. The Queen also gave him certain monopolies and the confiscated estates of noblemen in both England and Ireland, and he found himself able to send out a colony at his own expense. The Queen would not let her favorite run the risk of getting killed and thrown overboard by Spaniards; but Raleigh, though he did not himself go, sent out two ships which sailed April 27, 1584, to discover and explore the

P

coast of North America northward from Florida.
He did not know then that the Spaniards had
already sailed along the coast as far as the Chesapeake Bay.

The road to the West Indies in those days lay in
creeping along the coast of Europe and Africa to
the Canary Islands and then striking out boldly
westward.   Instead of following a short straight line
— the modern ocean lane, two miles wide — they
moved first down, and then up, over half a circle.
One month's sailing brought Raleigh's ships to the
Antilles, June 20th.   Then moving northward, on
the 4th of July they reached the American coast,
from which the land breeze wafted the delicious
perfume of blooming flowers.

Yet the ships could not get into the country,
because they were not able to find an inlet.   This
seems strange to us who can see along the coast, on
our well-made maps, all sorts of estuaries, bays, and
arms of the sea.   They sailed one hundred and
twenty miles and then entered the first opening
visible, which was probably New Inlet, in North
Carolina.   In the name of England's Queen, they
took possession of the inviting land, which was very
sandy and low toward the water's edge.   Grapes
were so plentiful that the very beating and surge of
the sea overflowed them.   Coming out of England,
then a very bleak land compared with its garden-

like surface as seen to-day, these men were pleased
with the richness of this southern landscape and
archipelago. The forests were full of deer, rabbits,
hares, and birds in incredible abundance. Of trees
they noticed the pine, cedar, cypress, sassafras, and
others.

The war chief of the country, with forty or fifty
men who seemed to have very good manners, came
to meet them. The English asked the name of the
country. The savage, who did not understand the
question, said, "Win-gan-da-coa," which means, "you
wear fine clothes." The Englishman, supposing
that the Indian had replied to his question, thought
that "Win-gan-da-coa" was the name of the country.
Many geographical names in all parts of the world
have arisen in this same way, when exchange of
ideas is by signs only.

The next day the chief brought his wife and
children to make a call on the white visitors. This
American lady had a band of white coral on her
forehead and strings of pearls hanging down from
her ears to her waist. The other women wore earrings of copper, and the king had a plate of metal
on his head. The men wore their hair long on one
side, but the women on both sides. Captain Bar-
low, with seven men, went twenty miles to Roanoke
Island, where they found a village of nine houses
built of cedar and fortified round about with sharp-

pointed trees, with the entrance narrow and easily defended. Here they were entertained by the chief's wife.

Pleased and happy though they were with the air and the soil, the trees, the fruits, and the people, Raleigh's pioneers were not very practically minded about either exploration or colonization. After a few weeks they returned to England, taking with them two natives, one of them named Wanchese and the other Manteo, after whom the town in Dare County is named.

Raleigh was delighted with the results of the voyage, and the Queen even more so. She made her favorite a knight, so that ever afterwards he was called Sir Walter Raleigh. She felt that her reign was honored by the discovery. She gave the new country a name which showed that she was still unmarried. The state of Virginia is the oldest child, the first born of the noble family of English-speaking commonwealths. Raleigh had a new seal of his arms cut, showing that he was the warden and governor of the land of the Virgin Queen. He became a member of Parliament from Devon, and secured political advantages which still further enriched him. He now dreamed of ruling a great estate beyond sea in semi-feudal style.

Raleigh sent a squadron of seven ships, which sailed in the spring of 1585. On board were one hundred English and Irish householders, with many things necessary to begin a new state, but without one woman. Such a " colony " might make a camp, but never a home. It was under the charge of Ralph Lane, who had, like Raleigh, seen service in Ireland, and whom many Irishmen followed to the new world. Thomas Cavendish, who afterwards sailed round the world, Hariot the mathematician who developed the science of algebra, and the artist White, a good painter, who engaged to make water colors of what he saw, were of the number.

The seven ships went out ready either to fight or to trade with Spaniards, on their long round-about way from the Canaries to the West Indies. In due season the squadron dropped anchors off the little sand-spit between Pamlico Sound and Ocacroke Inlet.

What happened to Raleigh's colonies in North Carolina belongs not to this our story of the " Romance of Discovery," but to our succeeding volume of " The Romance of Colonization." Suffice it to say, that in March, 1586, Sir Ralph Lane explored the Roanoke River in search of gold mines and an entrance into the Pacific Ocean. He and his men were driven back by hunger after having eaten their dogs. The colony was a total failure. Visited by Sir Francis Drake, who had been in the West Indies attacking the Spanish settlements, the colonists returned on his ships, reaching Plymouth, July 27, 1586.

Robbing Spaniards had thus far paid better than planting colonies. Though Raleigh's venture had not been a success, yet there was much to please the Queen, the Court, and himself. Thomas Hariot the mathematician, and the man who had best used his eyes and pen, brought back a good description of the country, and this, John White, the skilful artist, had illustrated in water colors; for, at that time, there was scarcely an oil-painter in all England unless it were a Dutchman or Italian.

Among other things, the potato was carried into Ireland by the Irishmen. The tubers were first planted on Raleigh's estate, and in time formed the national vegetable of Ireland. They served also to enrich the British table, for at this time garden vegetables were little known or used in England by the common folks, who in winter lived wholly on salt meat, fish, and grain. Royalty and the nobles had to depend on the Dutch. The island of Walcheren in Zealand was called " Queen Elizabeth's kitchen garden." Then there were Indian corn and tobacco. The dried weed made a great sensation and became very popular, even the game or joke of weighing smoke getting into vogue. The Dutchmen took to pipes and cigars even more than the English.

Another Virginian enterprise was planned. With eighty-nine men, seventeen women, and two children, a second settlement was begun July 22, 1587. A little babe, the first child born of English parents in America, saw the light on the 18th of August, and was named Virginia. Her mother was the daughter of the governor, John White. Dare County was named after her father. Late in the autumn, Governor White returned to England for provisions and reinforcements; but owing to the war excitement in England on account of the Spanish Armada, no help ever reached the colonists, most of whom miserably perished.

The first English colony in America was a failure, because of inexperience and a badly chosen place of settlement; but, more than all, on account of the war with Spain. It added a little, but only a little, to geographical knowledge; yet, nevertheless, it was Raleigh, who by talking and writing, by his money, his energy, and his practical experiments, educated Englishmen into the idea of building up a nation beyond the sea.

When the seventeenth century opened, not only had England failed to hold a foot of land in the new world, but it seemed as though Spain alone would dominate the entire continent. Who then could foresee that great family of English-speaking nations in both hemispheres and on five continents, which are now bound together by a common language, hope, and idea? If England is to be honored above all countries on earth as the mother of commonwealths, Raleigh is the first and greatest of foster-fathers.

CHAPTER XXI.

CAPTAIN JOHN SMITH EXPLORES VIRGINIA AND THE NEW ENGLAND COAST.

THE settlement of Jamestown belongs to the romance of colonization, and not to that of discovery and exploration. Nevertheless, Captain John Smith was an English explorer and adventurer, rather than a colonizer. He was such a great romancer and even so much of a falsifier, that it is very uncertain whether he ever was in Hungary fighting the Turks, as he declared he had been. It is, however, an historical fact, that he gained his experience in war, as did every one of the military fathers and protectors of the American colonies, in the Dutch war of independence. Captain John Smith served four years in the army of the Dutch United States against Spain.

Arriving at Jamestown, when about thirty years old, he was taken prisoner while exploring the Chickahominy. He was brought by Opecancanough, whose name remains on a Virginia river,— the Opecan,—to Powhattan, a war chief whose town was on the York River. After a few weeks Smith was released with presents of corn for the colonists. He made a boating voyage, as much for food as for knowledge, up the James River as far as Richmond, all the while, no doubt, having the hope of striking upon some passage into China.

In 1608 he made two extended surveys of the Chesapeake Bay and its tributary waters. He probably entered the Susquehanna, the Potomac, and the Potapsco rivers, and looked upon the site of Baltimore. He heard of the dreaded Mohawks, — a tribe of the Iroquois whose power extended from Canada to the Carolinas, and from the Connecticut to the Mississippi, and with whom Champlain in Canada and La Salle in Illinois, as we have seen, had already come in contact. Captain Smith made a map of his discoveries, which is still very interesting. He saw from the first that the only thing to make colonies successful was intelligently directed labor, good agriculture, and manual industry. Gold-seeking meant the chase of phantoms, followed by starvation and death. He left the colony in September, 1610. but whether for his own or the colony's good, or both, it is not certain.

In 1614, having noticed that "the Dutch had become rich by the contemptible trade of fish," and had thus beaten even the Spaniards in acquiring wealth, so that the powerful monarchy had to make truce with the little republic, Smith got London

merchants to fit out for him two ships with which
to open the mines of wealth in the ocean. Coming
over to the coast of North America, he kept his
men busy in fur-trading and fishing, whereby he
and they made plenty of money, and at the same
time he explored a considerable part of the coast of
our three eastern states, Maine, New Hampshire,
and Massachusetts. He made a pretty fair map of
the country named New England, and sent copies
to his friend Henry Hudson. For his services, he
was given the rank of admiral.

In June, 1615, he tried to establish a small colony
in Maine, but storms prevented this. He was captured by a French man-of-war, but escaped in a
boat. From 1616 to 1631 he wrote books and
pamphlets, showing his countrymen their grand
opportunity, and urging the colonization of America. He also narrated his own adventures on the
European continent, many of which, as he relates
them, are now believed to be fictitious. With all
his faults, Captain John Smith must be ranked
among the first of the English explorers of America.

When the Pilgrim fathers and mothers, who had
been reinforced and tempered in republican Holland, landed on Plymouth Rock to lay the foundations of distinctive America, the original work done
by English explorers on the Atlantic coast had been
neither large, nor important, nor brilliant. Except

the voyage of the Italian, Sebastian Cabot, along
the shore, and the entrance of some parties into a
few of the rivers, bays, and inlets, they had not discovered or explored any part of the coast not pre-
viously made known by either the Spanish or the
French, while the Dutch discovered and revealed
the coast line between Virginia and New England.
It was, however, reserved for the Englishman, last
in discovery, to be first in successful colonization.

CHAPTER XXII.

THE DUTCH ATTEMPT THE NORTHEAST PASSAGE AND OPEN THE SEAS OF THE ORIENT.

TO the day of his death, Columbus thought he had discovered only some islands off the coast of Japan. The aim of Cabot, Frobisher, Davis, and others, even into the seventeenth century, was to discover a passage to China either by the northwest or the southwest, or right through America. With pluck and perseverance, they kept on trying to find also the Northeast Passage. The southeast route around the Cape of Good Hope was already held by Portuguese, and, besides, it was exceedingly far off. The company of Merchant Adventurers, of which Sebastian Cabot in his old age became president, sent Sir Hugh Willoughby with three ships northward, but he never came back. Richard Chancellor, in another vessel, "discovered" Archangel and began direct trade with Russia. The Muscovy Company was formed in London. In 1556 the brave Stephen Burrough took his little English ships up as far as Nova Zembla, and partially explored it and the coasts adjacent, but came back with experience only. Once again, in 1580, the Englishmen tried again, only to be driven back by the frost king. After that, it was impossible to get English capitalists to advance money on any further experiment in finding the Northwest Passage to China. Failing again and again to cut through the continent, and losing money in the many attempts, they never got thoroughly interested in America until its commercial advantages had been demonstrated.

During the first age of exploration, the Dutch United States had not been able to join in adventures on the deep and distant seas. The little republic of seven states, which in 1579 formed their Union, and in 1581 published their Declaration of Independence, had but eight hundred thousand inhabitants, and was fighting for life against Spain. Their territory consisted chiefly of a narrow strip of fertile clay soil lying along the sea, between the Scheldt and the Ems rivers, with a large sand-heath and plenty of morasses over the rest of the national area, all of which was no larger than New Hampshire.

Every man, every ship, and every dollar had to be used to fight the Spaniards. At first the case seemed as hopeless as that of the shepherd boy of Bethlehem, armed only with five smooth stones and a sling, against the Philistine giant. Nevertheless, the Dutch, with genuine grit, with faith in God, with

intense hatred against the Inquisition, with enterprise and skill in trade, kept up the fight. They
paid their debts, especially the soldiers' wages, so
that their army never mutinied and the country
actually grew richer. Declaring war openly in an
honorable way, they enriched themselves by seizing
the Spanish treasure ships and by keeping up trade
with their enemies' countries and colonies even in
time of war. One admiral, Piet Hein, captured the
Silver Fleet, containing twelve millions of dollars.

When the English abandoned the bold but dis-
appointing work in the North Sea, the Dutch resolved to find the northern route to China. The
first proposition of the sort had come to them, in
1581, from the English sea-captain, Beets, but was
then necessarily refused. Gradually, however, the
idea of beating Spain at sea and compelling her to
sue for peace, became popular and was made very
effective. By the end of the century, having begun
the war in 1567, they sent out Dutch ships and men
to plant colonies in the world at large, which had
been divided up by the Pope, between the Spaniards
and Portuguese.

The Dutch government had not begun hostilities
against the Spaniards in any mean or underhanded
way, by privateering, piracy, or buccaneering, but in
open war honorably declared, and when they made
truce with the Spaniards in 1609 they kept it in

good faith. Their rulers were not vacillating, now
approving and now disapproving of their captains
at sea as it suited their changing humors, but the
States-General or Congress, in 1614, publicly offered
a prize of twenty-five thousand guilders to any one
who would discover a northern passage to the
East Indies. To win the money, the navigator
must go and return. Dutch traders made expeditions among the icebergs, and opened a good business with those regions bordering on the White Sea
between Lapland and Russia, having their chief station at Archangel. The great commercial house of
de Moucheron, at Middleburg in Zealand, was especially famous for its wealth made in this way. As
early as 1598, it is said, Dutch ships and crews
were in the Hudson and Delaware rivers, but simply
as traders making no claim as discoverers.

Among the learned promoters of Dutch exploration was Domine Petrus Plancius, who besides being
a pastor and preacher was one of the best-informed
geographers in Europe. His writings and personal
influence greatly helped to send the ships of the
republic in all oceans. In 1594, 1595, and 1596,
brave soldiers and skilful pilots carried the orange,
white, and blue flag still farther northward and
eastward.

One of the most famous of these expeditions was
that of Heemskerk, Barentz, and Derijp, who were

sent out in 1596. They discovered Nova Zembla,
which is a pair of twin islands like those of Tsushima
between Japan and Korea, and also Spitsbergen.
Their ship was so frozen in, that they were obliged
to winter on Nova Zembla. They had plenty of
clothing, wine, and food, except meat. Using the
driftwood, they constructed a hut with a big fire-
place. The white polar bears prowled about them,
evidently longing to taste the Dutchmen, who shot
Bruin and used his fat to feed their lamps, which
were kept burning during the perpetual night from
November 4 to January 24.

These merry Dutchmen, in the white world of
ice and snow and far from their homes, celebrated
with fun and frolic their old home-land festival on
the 5th of January — the eve of the day of the
Three Kings — by tossing the pancake and drinking healths to their boatswain, who acted for the
nonce as sovereign of Nova Zembla. When daylight came, the bears left and the foxes came in
troops, furnishing the men with fresh and whole-
some meat, and with material for caps and socks.
In June, fearing lest they might be again shut in
by the ice, they left their ship among the bergs.
In two open boats, and despite many perils and
labors, they reached Norway and home, where they
were welcomed as men risen from the dead. Their
story has often been told and sung by prose writers

and poets. They were proud of having gone further than the Englishmen, but their awful experiences dampened for a long time any zeal for further explorations. Within the present century, the relics of Barentz and his men have been found and placed in the Rijks Museum at Amsterdam, where to-day they are eloquent and compel tears.

The story of these Arctic explorers was well known in England. We find it referred to on the theatre stage. Shakespeare in "Twelfth Night," Act III., Scene II., makes Fabian in Olivia's house say to Sir Andrew Ague-cheek, "You are now sailed into the North of my lady's opinion; where you will hang like an icicle on a Dutchman's beard."

Nevertheless, the Hollanders were not discouraged. They turned their thoughts in other directions and to warmer regions, being determined that the Spaniards and Portuguese should not monopolize trade with the far East. When Cornelius Houtman of Gouda, — famous for its pipes and printing, — who had spent some years at Lisbon, came back and told of the tremendous profits made by the Portuguese in spices, the desire to have a hand in the trade was strong. By the advice of Domine Plancius, nine Dutch merchants formed a company and at once fitted out at their own cost four vessels which cleared from the Texel, April 2, 1595, for Ban-

tam and Java — names now associated with diminu-
tive chickens and good coffee. After fighting storms,
Portuguese, and tropical diseases, ninety brave men,
out of the two hundred and fifty who started
out, returned to Amsterdam in 1597, with enough
pepper, nutmeg, and mace to lower at once the
high prices of spices. There was a general jubilee
all over Holland. The Dutch had invaded Portugal's half of the world.

The great obstacle to the navigation of Eastern
seas was the want of charts and geographical knowledge. Yet even this was soon overcome. There
was a Dutchman named Jan van Linschoten born
in Haarlem in 1563. He had two brothers in Spain
established in business, which, in 1586, the King of
Spain broke up, by seizing Dutch ships, and order-
ing all trade with the heretics to be stopped. The
young Haarlemer entered the service of the Bishop
of Goa, when that Portuguese prelate went out to
India. Linschoten, in making this voyage, learned
the sea-route and methods of navigation and trade.
Having returned to his own country and while living at Enkhuizen, in 1592, he joined himself as a
trader, or supercargo, to one of the ships which,
in 1594, went through the Arctic seas to find the
way to India. Turned back by icebergs, he took a
great interest in the expedition of Heemskerk and
Barentz in 1596. In the same year, he published

his wonderful books which gave charts and told of
the sea-routes not only to the Spice Islands, but
even to the Chinese coasts, Formosa, and Japan.

Linschoten's writings opened to all Europe, but
especially to the Dutch and English, the whole
Eastern world.   He was treasurer of the city of
Enkhuizen, not then, as it is now, a sleepy little
town, but a great flourishing city with hundreds of
ships daily at its wharves.   His books treated of
the voyage of a mariner to the East or Portuguese
Indies, with descriptions of the cruises made by the
Portuguese in the East.   At last the "East Indies,"
so long talked about, were actually mapped and
described, and the way thither made clear; but the
Portuguese looked on the Dutchmen as burglars
who had broken into their secret house and rifled
their private papers.   Another volume described
the coast of Guinea and another the resources
of the King of Spain.   Linschoten's books were
quickly translated into Latin, French, English, and
German and had a tremendous effect.   Soon after
this, the Dutch East and West India companies
were organized, and also the English companies,
of the same name, which were copied after the
Dutch.

Linschoten's book gave the first true map of the
world in which the East India shores, islands, and
routes were accurately placed.   It made a deep

impression in England, where we find it made the
subject of a joke in the theatres. Marian, in Shakespeare's " Twelfth Night," Act III., Scene II., says of
Malvolio, after the latter had been misled by a false
letter into making love to Countess Olivia, " He
does smile his face into more lines than are in the
new map, with the augmentation of the Indies."
Another Dutchman, Gerard Mercator, by his globes
and maps, especially those drawn on what are called
" Mercator's projection," did more than any other
one person to set men's minds free from the ancient
and imperfect notions of Ptolemy, whose geography
had been rendered obsolete by the numerous discoveries of the sixteenth century.

After this, the orange, white, and blue flag of the
Dutch republic began to flutter in every sea, and
expeditions for trade and exploration were numerous. They examined the coasts of countries, like
India, which the Portuguese had possessed. The
Dutch established trading houses at a number of
points in Guinea and along the coast of Africa, and
in India, Malacca, Burma, Formosa, and Japan.
They discovered and explored the coasts of the
Malay Archipelago, New Holland now called Australia, New Zealand, and Tasmania or Van Die-
men's Land. The Dutch were the first to begin
studying the Oriental languages, and they founded
the first Asiatic society. In time, they conquered

the Spice Islands of the Malay Archipelago from the Portuguese.

Turning their attention to America, as early as 1598, they sent out an expedition westward, which sailed through Magellan's Straits and into the Pacific. A Dutchman from the city of Hoorn discovered and named Cape Horn. In later years they captured from the Spaniards some of the West India Islands, set up factories in Guiana and Brazil, explored the archipelago south and west of Patagonia, and repeatedly circumnavigated the world. No one would ever get any idea from a geography or atlas now published in England or the United States, how numerous were the discoveries and how great were the explorations which the Dutch made in every part of the world; for the British conquerors have erased or Anglicized most of the Dutch names formerly on the maps.

It was when in search of the Northwest Passage that Henry Hudson in the Dutch ship, *Half Moon*, —so named after a famous fortress of that name,— discovered and entered the Hudson River.

Undiscouraged by the English and Dutch attempts to reach China by sailing around Russia and Siberia, Hudson resolved again to dare the terrors of the ice and snows. His whole mature life had been spent on icy seas. In 1607, being employed by the Muscovy Company, in a little ship with only ten men, he had reached within ten degrees of the pole. In 1608 he had sailed as far as Nova Zembla. When he came back, the Amsterdam Dutchmen, eager to find some one of experience and ability who would try once again to win the golden prize of twenty-five thousand guilders, were ready to employ Hudson in the new venture. At first the merchants and the sea-captain could not agree on terms, and for a while it looked as if the French envoy in the Netherlands would get Hudson into French service; but on the 8th of January, 1609, Captain Hudson and his friend Hondius, the famous map-maker who could talk both Dutch and English, met and agreed. Hudson soon informed the French minister that he could not serve King Henry IV.

The directors of the East India Company contracted with Hudson to fit out a vessel of sixty tons' burden for a voyage, around the north of Nova Zembla, to India. It was while Hudson was waiting for the sailing of his ship, that the English refugees escaping from persecution, and destined to found Massachusetts, arrived in Amsterdam from Scrooby, England. Some of them may have seen him sail away, for it is very probable that they lived in the neighborhood of the wharves. Plancius and Linschoten, no doubt, helped Hudson with advice and maps.

On the fourth day of April, the *Half Moon* swung clear from her moorings, within the half-moon canal at Amsterdam and in front of the Weeper's Tower, — which old building is still standing, and contains the harbor master's office. About and in front of this tower, on both sides of the canal, were gathered the women, children, and friends of the hardy Dutch mariners about to sail on adventurous voyages. Then, and afterwards, during the next fifty years, many crowds assembled here to see ships sailing for America. Hudson, passing out into the Zuyder Zee and up through the Texel, was soon in the North, butting against the great ice mass that refused to open or to allow him to reach Nova Zembla. It was quite soon evident that he could not find India that year by going eastward. What should he do?

CHAPTER XXIII.

HUDSON'S crew consisted of but twenty men. Like himself, the sailors did not want to go home empty-handed. So he gave them a choice of two routes in seeking the Northwest Passage. The first was by sailing about the latitude of forty degrees. This course would bring them to a warm and comfortable climate. Or, they might sail through Davis Strait and inside the Arctic circle. In either case he hoped to reach the Orient.

Although the crew voted to try the Davis Strait passage, yet, either on account of storms which drove him out of his course, or else because he deliberately chose to try a more southern passage, Hudson moved southwestwardly. He soon reached Newfoundland, sailed down along the coast of Maine, and stopped at Mount Desert Island, where he cut down and trimmed a huge tree to make a new foremast. He came to Cape Cod, which he named New Holland. Getting far out beyond the sands and shallows, he did not see the coast again until the 28th of August, when he found himself off the coast of Maryland. Moving northward alongshore, he entered Delaware Bay, and coasted along and around New Jersey.

On Wednesday, September 2, 1609, at five o'clock in the afternoon, he passed around Sandy Hook. Charmed with the scenery, he cast his anchor in what he thought was a great lake of water. He was in New York Bay, where for ten days he remained, keeping his men meanwhile busy in making soundings, locating the channel, and exploring the bay beyond the narrows. He invited the Indians to come on board his ship and treated them well, but in the trip beyond the narrows, Coleman, one of his crew, was shot by the red men. He traded off axes, knives, shovels, and other tools or trifles for furs. The savages made ornaments of whatever could be scoured and kept bright. At last, believing it was safe to do so, he took his ship up into this waterway, which he thought might possibly lead toward China, if not to it. Passing what is now the Battery, he sailed up along Manhattan Island, the Palisades, the Highlands, the Catskills, and reached the vicinity of Troy about the 20th of September. This was what we call the head of navigation, and the water was too shallow to allow further progress. Hudson sent a ship's boat about twenty-seven miles northward beyond the anchorage. The men found the river still more shallow, and the volume of water growing less, with a great mountainous country lying beyond.

This was a sad disappointment to Hudson and his crew, after they had sailed nearly one hundred and fifty miles through so noble a stream. Much of the water was salt or brackish until past the Highlands, and hence they supposed that they were in a strait, rather than a river flowing out of springs in the mountains and therefore entirely landlocked. There was no getting to China that way. On the 23d of September they turned their prow southward and after eleven days sailed out from Sandy Hook.

Thus, for over a month, amid the autumnal glories of nature's colors, the orange, white, and blue flag of the federal republic of the Netherlands had been mirrored on the grandest river in eastern North America. The brave Hollanders and their English captain had revealed a new coast, river, and territory between New England and Virginia.

Instead of going, as most vessels would have done, to the West Indies or the Canary Islands, the *Half Moon* moved straight across the ocean, arriving November 7, 1609, at Dartmouth. At first, the Englishmen wanted to claim the credit of this discovery. They detained both ship and captain, and the *Half Moon* did not get to Amsterdam till July of the new year. The British government permitted Hudson to keep his contract with his Dutch employers and send on his report to Amsterdam, yet Hudson himself probably never got to Holland again. Nevertheless, Henry Hudson had discovered for the Dutch the greatest of all the gateways, from the Atlantic into the heart of the region which is now United States territory.

The next year, with English sailors, Hudson started again to sail through America to China. He entered and explored the great bay which is named after him. Then his crew mutinied, and putting him with his son and seven infirm sailors in an open boat, set them adrift amid the floating ice. So ended his useful and daring life.

Strangely enough, Champlain, the French explorer, as well as Hudson visited Mount Desert Island, in 1609, and thence moved northward and into the St. Lawrence, while Hudson went southward and into the waterway of the Empire State. Within four months of time and two degrees of latitude, they were near each other in the territory of New York, Champlain being at Ticonderoga and Hudson at Troy. It was like the nearness and farness of de Soto and Coronado in the Mississippi valley.

The actions of Champlain and Hudson were initial, typical, and far-reaching in influence upon the decision of the question which occupied states-

men, armies, and nations from 1609 until 1763.
That question was, whether Latin or Germanic
civilization should prevail in North America. The
French were a military people, bound by Church
and State to mediæval and feudal ideas. The
Dutch were commercial, republican, and full of
modern and progressive ideas. The Hurons and
Algonquins became allies of the French. The Iroquois from the year 1609 sought the Dutch and
remained their friends and helpers. In the long
struggle that followed, first the Iroquois, then the
Dutch, and finally the English prevailed. The tri-
color flag, with all it meant of hope for freedom and
republican government still remains, though Indian,
Dutch, French, or British power in the Hudson
valley is no more.

Hudson had discovered new coasts, — those of
our Middle States from the tip of Delaware to
nearly the northern end of New York. He had
found a great river and its tributaries, and had told
of the men, animals, and wonderful products seen
by him. Immediately the desire to get the furs
in this new market became a passion; for the
Dutch lived in a cold damp country, and peltry
was ever in great demand. Since the trade with
Archangel in Russia had been shut off, the Dutchmen were very glad to find in the new world what
seemed to be a market; where, instead of hard

money, they need only pay in beads, trinkets, axes, and knives, while the supply of furs appeared to be inexhaustible. A trading company had already been formed, and no sooner did the *Half Moon* sail into the river Y at Amsterdam on her return, than the directors engaged the Dutch mate and a number of the crew to make another trip to America. With others, these men who had seen America started off again. Entering the Hudson River, they met the redskins coming off in their canoes with bundles of beaver skins and other furs. On their breasts dangled the various bits of hardware which Hudson had bartered on his first voyage. Even shovel blades had become jewellery.

All Holland was soon stirred up on the subject of furs and exploration. Here was a market as good as China, but much nearer home. The merchants living in Rotterdam, Hoorn, and Enkhuizen, demanded of their state legislatures and the Dutch Congress all information possible about the new country, and to have the charts of the South, or Delaware, River, and the North, or Hudson, River published. The facts in hand were duly forthcoming and the region was named New Netherland.

Note this name. It was not New Netherlands. The Dutch were now a nation, with one country, and not merely a collection of provinces. New Netherland meant unity. It was the token of vic-

ARRIVAL OF THE "HALF MOON" AT THE HUDSON RIVER.

tory over Spain, and another way of translating their national motto *Eendracht maakt Macht*, or " Union makes strength."

In the year 1612 five ships were despatched for further exploration and trade. Among the officers of these ships were Henry Christiansen, Adriaen Block, and Cornelius Jacobson May. Two of these names are preserved in Block Island and Cape May. On their return home, besides a cargo of peltry, they brought two sons of war chiefs, whom they named Valentine and Orson. These young Indians were taken around through the different Dutch provinces, and the sight of them excited a tremendous interest in the New Netherland beyond sea.

The year 1609 was the first one of the Great Truce. Spain had been trying during forty-three years to conquer the United States of the Netherlands, but had not succeeded. She had already buried tens of thousands of her sons and mercenaries in the Dutch ditches, but the men who fought for freedom were very tough, brave, and skilful, and were growing richer and stronger every day. Spain, fearing exhaustion, had to ask for peace, which was finally granted, after the owner of Peru and Mexico had recognized the Dutch Congress or States-General as "their High Mightinesses."

By the terms of this truce, however, the Dutch

could not in honor begin a colony in New Netherland; for it would have been against their treaty
to have then settled the country and occupied it.
The Dutch kept good faith with Spain. Tolerant
and ready to welcome men who worshipped God
in whatever way pleasing to them, provided they
obeyed the laws of the republic, the Dutch government gave asylum and welcome to Jews, Roman
Catholics, the Anabaptists (so-called), the Walloons
and French Huguenots, and to the Pilgrim Fathers,
mothers and children, and to many other religious
refugees driven out from England. Yet to send
a colony to America, in dominions still claimed by
Spain, would have been an act of war.

Yet, all the time the Dutchmen kept talking
about New Netherland, as well as their other conquests and discoveries. It is true that Barneveldt,
the Arminian political party, and the ultra-State-
Sovereignty men opposed the idea of colonization,
but the majority of people and the National party,
or the Calvinists, led by Prince Maurice, heartily
favored planting a Dutch colony in New Netherland. Jesse de Forest of Leyden was one of thousands who looked forward to the time when, the
truce being over, they could occupy the American
Netherland with farmers as well as traders and
build towns and cities. Barneveldt, the great statesman and diplomatist, feared that the Dutch people

might be led away by military ambition, while Maurice, the President or Stadtholder and head of the army, and the Dutch people in general, especially their ministers, geographers, and navigators, eagerly hoped to see the region about the Delaware and Hudson rivers become a New Holland. Although the Dutch could not then colonize Manhattan Island, they built huts where the sailors might find shelter and get fresh water and provisions.

Captain Christiansen sailed with Block in 1613, — the one in the *Fortune* (or *Good Tidings*), the other in the *Tiger*, — and, landing on Manhattan Island, made it the centre of the fur-trade with the Indians. He determined to remain with his men through the winter and some time later, and so these first white inhabitants on the site of New York City built houses there, using the tree-trunks for posts, making the walls of boards, and roofing and covering them with the bark of trees peeled off in great masses.

The Dutch were something more than mere traders. They were true explorers, having a real desire to add to the science of geography which was so richly cultivated in their native country. The names of their countrymen, Plancius, Linschoten, Mercator, and Wagenaar, were already honorably known throughout all the civilized world. We do not find the level-headed Dutchmen digging for

R

gold or searching for a passage to China, but engaging industriously in honest trade. From his
abode on Manhattan Island, Christiansen, in his
boats, explored the numerous and wonderful waterways which lead to the island whereon is America's
greatest city.

After making himself acquainted with that wonderful system of waterways which makes New York
Bay the greatest of all the gateways from the Atlantic into the continent, Christiansen took his ship,
Good Tidings (or *Good Fortune*, as we may translate
the name), up to the great northern centre of Indian
trade. This was at the junction of the Mohawk
and the Hudson rivers, where the Indian trails from
the north, west, east, and south came together.
Here, also, the converging waterways and the valleys,
with the wonderful configuration of the country,
make one of the most interesting strategic points
in the eastern United States. Nowhere else on the
continent, from Labrador to Alabama, does the great
Appalachian chain of mountains sink so low, forming a great natural gateway between New England and the West. From the St. Lawrence River
to Sandy Hook, there is a great rift valley and a
natural waterway, which crosses the land highways
between the rising and setting sun. The railways
of to-day from the north, south, east, and west
(except that through the Hoosac Tunnel), do but

follow the Indian trails once made for the moccasin. The steamboats run in the old water-paths of the canoe.

There was not at this time a more intellectual or keen-witted people in all Europe than the brave republicans of Holland. They were daring, enterprising, and resourceful. Their universities so far surpassed those of Great Britain that thousands of English and Scottish students attended at Leyden, Utrecht, Harderwijk, and Groningen. Those who look at the Dutch through the spectacles of English or sectional American prejudice make a great mistake. Such people cannot properly understand either Netherlandish or American history.

When the winter was over, Christiansen chose Barren Island, in the middle of the Hudson River, as his headquarters. Here he built a fort, the first in New Netherland, which he named Nassau, after Maurice, Count of Nassau, the great defender of the Dutch Union and the patron of exploration and of colonies. The lordly river which Hudson had entered was now named Mauritius. Barren Island near Albany, like Barren Hill near Philadelphia and several other very fertile places in the United States, was named after the bears. Both island and hill are on rich soil and are well covered with trees.

After making further explorations, Christiansen was killed by Orson, one of the two Indians who

had been in Holland, though we do not know why.
The command of the fort then fell upon Jacob
Eelkins, who for three or four years remained at
the head of the station. He found the Iroquois
exceedingly anxious to buy firearms, and learned
that they came from long distances westward to
get them. At that time, no better guns were made
anywhere else in Europe than in Holland. The
musketeers of Holland and other cities constantly
practised at the butts, or *doelen*, and the Dutch were
superb marksmen. The evolution of the firearm
from the heavy arquebus to the modern musket was
proceeding rapidly. Most old English words refer-
ring to a gun, especially to the firing part, and the
lock and cock, are of Dutch origin.

The later explorations of the Mohawk valley, by
Arendt van Curler, revealed the wonderful canoe
route and waterway between the East and the West,
connecting the Great Lakes with the Hudson. The
water passage and land routes northward to New
France had been of old used by the Iroquois. In subsequent years Dutchmen explored all New Jersey,
eastern Pennsylvania, and Delaware. Coming up
the Susquehanna valley, they first entered that
wonderful lake country of fifteen or more bodies of
water in central New York, from Oneida Lake to
Silver Lake, containing rich forests full of fur-bear-
ing animals.

Thus, from its outskirts to the far interior, the whole of New Netherland, the empire region, which afterward became our four Middle States, was explored, and Dutch maps made of the region thus discovered and opened. One of the most noted maps, of 1614–15, which shows the country from Rhode Island to the Delaware River, is remarkable for its knowledge of interior New York. It proves what Christiansen and Block did to make known America beyond the seacoast. In a word, the Dutchmen, although they had not yet settled a colony, as the English had done at Jamestown, did greatly enlarge European knowledge of the resources of the continent and of its physical geography.

CHAPTER XXIV.

LET us see now what became of Captain Adriaen
Block. While his comrade, Christiansen, was
up in the Mohawk region, Block's ship, *Tiger*, caught
fire and was burned to the water's edge; but, undis-
mayed, though with few and poor tools, and using
chiefly the green wood of the forest, he built the
first ship constructed on Manhattan Island, and
christened it the *Onrust* (*Restless*). The little ship
was launched in the springtime and made a splendid record. Being only sixteen tons' burden, Block
could take her into the rivers and streams where
a larger vessel could not go.

He first went up the East River to Hell Gate
and threaded his way among the islands into Long
Island Sound, which he explored on its northern
shore. He passed a large river, to the region or
valley of which he, or some later Dutchman, gave
the name "Woesten Hoek," which means the corner or place of the wilderness. In the Indian
tongue, and as pronounced by the red man's lips,

when the English inquired its name. "Woesten Hoek" became "Housatonic." In one of the first large inlets, which was afterwards called New Haven harbor, he named the high ground Rodenburg, or Red Hill, the appropriateness of which any one will recognize who knows the vicinity of New Haven. He sailed into the Connecticut River and when he tasted the water, finding it so different from the brackish waters near New York and around Manhattan Island, he named it the Fresh River. The stream flowing into New Haven harbor he named the river of the Red Hill. He located the country of the Mohicans, and finding another river of sweet water, most probably the Pawtucket, he marked it on his map as being fresh. Then noticing the coast bend away to the northward, he steered over to an island rising out of the sea, which he called Block Island, which name it bears to-day. He probably explored the coast as far as Point Judith. Either he or later Dutchmen gave the region the name of Red Island, or Rood Eylandt, which in English is pronounced Rhode Island. The result of Block's explorations was to show that the land stretching out eastward from New York was an island.

He now entered Narragansett Bay, and finding it large and roomy, with a broad outlook, he named it Nassau Bay. He gave names to several more of the islands, and then passed along that tremendous extension of Massachusetts, east of Buzzard's Bay, which looks like a doubled-up arm as though this grand state was showing the thickness of her muscle. As in the geography, so in the seal and arms of the commonwealth, above the standing Indian, is the bent arm sheathed in armor. The Dutch skipper rounded Cape Cod and then struck over to the opposite coast, reaching Nahant, Marblehead harbor, and Salem Inlet, which he called Pye Bay.

Nearly all of Block's discoveries have been ruthlessly wiped out or altered by English settlers except the name of the island which he discovered. In Narragansett Bay, between Kingston County and Jamestown, is the little Dutch Island.

Captain May, whose vessel had been fitted out at Hoorn, the town which sent out both the ship and the man who discovered and named Cape Horn in South America, had taken the *Fortune* and had explored the southern coast of Long Island, which he found to be twenty-five Dutch miles long, from Visscher's Hoek, now called Montauk Point, to Manhattan Island. Visscher's name survives in an altered form in Fisher's Island, which belongs to New York. May also went along the coast of New Jersey, and he or later Dutchmen named Cape May and Cape Henlopen. The latter is the namesake

of a pretty little town called Hindeloopen, or the
running hind, which nestles behind the dikes of
the Zuyder Zee.

When Block started for Manhattan, he met the
ship *Fortune*, in command of Cornelius Hendrikson,
on its way to Holland.   He exchanged ships, direct-
ing Hendrikson to continue the double business of
trading for furs and making geography, while he
crossed the Atlantic to report the explorations of
himself, of Christiansen, and of May.   These reports
with the "figurative map" he laid before the government, which sat in the district of The Hague,
where the Congress of the United States sat.

In March of this very year, the Dutch Congress,
to stimulate enterprise and promote exploration, had
issued a general charter for those who "discovered
new passages, havens, countries, or places." Each
discoverer was to be rewarded by being given a
monopoly of trade to the country he should discover, during at least four voyages.   He was required within fourteen days from the return from
his first voyage to give his report, with exact details
of the work which he had accomplished.

It was on October 11, 1614, that Block presented
himself before the States-General, in one of those
rooms which overlook the Binnenhof in The Hague.
There he was able to prove that he had added vastly
to Henry Hudson's discovery and had opened new

countries. What Block showed was so far beyond what Captain John Smith had yet discovered, that a resolution was moved and carried to grant a charter to a company of merchants, which, some months before, on the 18th of July, had asked for the privilege of exclusive trade with America and Africa. Block's arguments won the day, and the charter was signed and sealed before sundown. In token of the unity of the United States of the Netherlands, — *e pluribus unum*, — the new region was called officially not New Netherlands, as most English writers have it, but New Netherland.

Curiously enough, on that same day, Captain John Smith, in England, was showing Prince Charles his journal and map of the region between Penobscot Bay and Cape Cod. He who became King Charles I. proposed the name New England, which was given. In Block's idea, New Netherland extended from the forty-fifth degree of north latitude to the Penobscot, beyond which was New France.

Meanwhile the Dutch, who were getting acquainted with the interior of northern New York, kept up their fort on Castle Island, in the Hudson, until a flood in 1617 nearly ruined it. Then Eelkins selected a spot at the junction of Norman's Kill with the Hudson River. This beautiful winding stream took its name from a Northman or Scandinavian who had cultivated land there. The Indian name was Tawasentha, meaning the place of many dead. For many generations this spot had been sacred as being not only their burying-place, but the eastern limit of the Iroquois confederacy. Near by rose a hill on the northern bank, called Tawas-gunshee, whence a view over the river valley could be obtained. Here the next year, in 1618, was held a great council of the five Indian tribes of the confederacy, whose long house, or residence, extended from the falls of Cohoes to those of Niagara. With solemn ceremonies, these senators of the forest formed, with the commander and officers of the Fort Nassau, a treaty of friendship and an alliance of mutual helpfulness. This league of peace, between the Dutch and Indians, became, in the course of American history, one of the primal elements which decided the fate of this continent for Anglo-Saxon civilization. Like a great dike, against which the waves of French energy and ambition beat in vain, it stood until the Indian ceased to be a political factor in the struggle. After Eelkins, it was remade and ratified by Arendt van Curler. It became that "silver chain" which was never broken until the English-speaking white men themselves quarrelled and separated.

The two significant ceremonies were the burial of the war-hatchet and the mutual drinking of the smoke of peace. The Indians laid a tomahawk upon the loose ground and the chiefs repeatedly trampled and trod it down, pushing earth over it until it was no longer visible. Then the calumet or pipe was filled with tobacco, passed around, and solemnly smoked by red and white men.

There are few more interesting historic sites in America than Tawasentha, near Albany. Here, according to Indian tradition, was the seat of the labors of their culture-hero Hiawatha, whom Longfellow has celebrated. Not far away lived and wrought the Indian's friend, Arendt van Curler, one of America's great men. He was so true a friend of the Five Nations, that they named the governors of New York after him — Corlear. The "Covenant of Corlear," so often referred to in Indian oratory, is not yet forgotten. Even the title which the Canadian Iroquois to this day give Queen Victoria, the Empress of India, is "The Great Curler" (Kora Kowa). The Iroquois, who hated Champlain, called the body of water in northern New York, Corlear's Lake, and the bay near which he was drowned in 1657, Corlear's Bay.

The little ship *Restless* was not yet at the end of its career of usefulness. In 1615, Captain Cornelius Hendrikson sailed in her around the coast of New Jersey. To one place he gave the name Eyerhaven, that is the haven of eggs, which is correct old English as well as good Dutch. It is now called Egg Harbor. He gave the name Henlopen to what is now called Cape May, and to the point opposite, Cape Cornelius, though these names were afterwards changed. He went up into the beautiful Delaware Bay, until he found that, like that which Hudson had discovered, it narrowed and became a river. In sailing up past where Philadelphia now is, he reached perhaps as far as Trenton. He or some one after him named the Delaware's principal affluent, the Schuylkill, that is, the hidden kill or stream.

The Great Truce was to end in 1621, and then war with Spain would begin again, and the Dutch would have opportunity to colonize New Netherland, if they wanted to. Yet there was little inducement to a Dutchman to leave his home permanently. For discovery or exploration, trade or commerce, thousands of young Dutchmen, brave, enterprising, and brainy, were ready to sail into any seas or to go to either pole, but not to stay forever away from their homeland. There was plenty of room in the republic and no overcrowding, for until 1620 there were less than a million people in the seven states of the Union.

Being a free land, where there was liberty of conscience for all men, there was no need of going elsewhere for worship in peace. The Dutch were not Pilgrims, because they had no need to be. Their

toleration and freedom had been already won.   Yet,
besides the Separatists, called Anabaptists, and the
Jews, driven out by the bigotry of persecuting state
churches, both Protestant and Catholic, there were
many Huguenots and British folks living in Holland.
These people were not rooted to the soil, but dwelt
as strangers in a strange land, whose language and
customs they but partially knew. It was easy for them
to go out as colonists to the new world, especially
when, if they returned home to England or France,
they would probably be at once clapped into prison.

When the Great Truce should be over in 1621,
there would be a fine opportunity for these Walloons
or French Protestants, or the English Separatists
from Yorkshire, to make homes in New Netherland.
By the year 1620, Barneveldt, who had opposed colonization, was dead, and the Arminian political party
or State-Sovereignty men had lost their power.
Maurice, the president of the republic of the Dutch
United States, received a petition from the directors of the New Netherland company who traded
with the Hudson River region and who now wanted
to colonize it. These gentlemen said that there
was an English preacher in Leyden who knew the
Dutch language very well, and who stated that not
fewer than four hundred families, both out of Holland and England, were inclined to go to New
Netherland to live.

The directors recommended that these people, who were no other than Rev. John Robinson, Elder Brewster, William Bradford, and the Pilgrim fathers, mothers, and children, should be aided in transporting themselves to America to settle in the Hudson River region. The directors had promised to give them free passage to America, and to furnish every family with cows and animals for their farms; but, as there was danger from their own cruel King James and from the Spaniards, they recommended that two ships of the Dutch navy be sent to convoy the squadron of colonists to New Netherland.

This petition of the Dutch directors looked very reasonable from the point of view of plain patriots and business men, or even of English refugees who wanted a home where the iron hands of the harsh kings, James I. of England and Philip III. of Spain, could not reach them. James, the fool-king, had put old Sir Walter Raleigh to death, and was now trying to make a match for his daughter with a Spanish prince. These Englishmen could not trust their "dread sovereign" not to harass or murder them.

To the political men in the States-General, however, the matter of helping English colonists who were under the ban of their bishops and politicians looked very different. Though the Dutch United States had declared themselves independent of Spain, and had won a twelve years' truce, their freedom was

not yet fully assured. Spain, now rich and strong
again, was to open a war next year, and every man
and ship, every pike, gun, and cartridge, were needed
for home defence. On the other hand, the Dutch
had defied and irritated King James, because this
monarch's intermeddling in Dutch affairs had become intolerable. They also had given offence to
the political church of England by harboring and
protecting the English refugees who were Separatists. The Dutch government had to be politic and
cautious. They tried to keep King James in good
humor, and professed to heed his remonstrances.
Indeed, they could not wholly break friendship
with the only other great Protestant Power in
Europe.

Furthermore, the English were already hinting at
and professing the preposterous claim that because
Henry Hudson was an Englishman, his discoveries
belonged to England, though he was a servant of
a Dutch company under the Dutch flag, and in a
Dutch ship with Dutch sailors. This same argu-
ment would have handed over the fruits of John and
Sebastian Cabot's discoveries to Italy. Still, while
there was even the shadow of a question, or an inch
of ground for the wavering British king to stand on,
it would have been the worst kind of policy for the
Dutch to send, as their first colony, a company of
people whom the English government and church

had persecuted and hated. It would have looked like open defiance.

So the States-General were obliged to deny the petition of the Dutch directors, and to disappoint the Pilgrims in their hope of settling in New Netherland under friendly and generous patronage and beneath a republican flag.

s

CHAPTER XXV.

WHEN the sixteenth century dawned, there were a good many motives to impel men to sail westward from Europe.

Besides the India spices and the American lodes, there were the vast treasures of the deep and the wealth in sea-food, which were not likely to be exhausted like gold or silver mines. The great currents coming up from the overheated water around the Equator and in the Gulf of Mexico is like the Nile River, which brings down out of the heart of Africa a top-dressing which enriches Egypt's fields. The Gulf Stream carries silt and animal life and matter, upon which the cod and other deep-sea fish feed, and makes a rich deposit on the Grand Banks off Newfoundland. Here during the ages billions of fish have accumulated in their generations, like mines in the water, storing up food for those nations of western Europe, whose religion requires the consumption of a great deal of fish on certain days.

Not only was it thought not the proper thing to

eat meat on Friday, but when the saints and holy days multiplied, there were at least three days in every week when fish dinners were necessary. This demand, both religious and commercial, gave the fishermen along the coast of France plenty to do, besides opportunities for wealth and stimulus to enterprise. It is highly probable that before the days of Columbus, French fishermen from St. Malo and Dieppe had sailed directly across the ocean and fished on the Grand Banks, without ever troubling their heads about exploration and geography.

After the different French provinces had become one great kingdom, and peace existed between the nations on either side of the Pyrenees, it was easy to send out Jacques Cartier, who entered the great river of St. Lawrence. He also ascended to Montreal and named it. Yet France furnished no important successors of Cartier in the line of exploration until, in Samuel Champlain, the man was found who began New France in America. Under the popular King Henry IV. the illustrious House of Bourbon was established on the throne of France.

The white lilies were the emblem of the Bourbons, and from 1689 to 1792 theirs was the flag of France. It was these white lilies that were borne with the stars and stripes to victory at Yorktown in 1781.

Champlain's first voyage was made in 1603. His explorations, begun in the region of the river and gulf of St. Lawrence, were continued during two summers along the coast of Maine. He entered the Penobscot and the Kennebec rivers and into Saco Bay. He visited Boston harbor, Cape Cod, and Nausett harbor, in what is now Massachusetts. In 1605, he again traversed the same line of summer exploration, making his maps in winter. A feeble colony had also been attempted on Nova Scotia. After three years and four months of noble pioneer exploration, Champlain reached France again to tell his story not only by word of mouth, but in books which were widely read and richly enjoyed.

When the colonists who had settled at Port Royal arrived at St. Malo early in October, and the specimens of grain, corn, wheat, rye, barley, oats, and other products were shown the king, Henry IV., His Majesty was greatly pleased. Champlain was made governor of another expedition sent out in 1608, when he laid the foundations of the city of Quebec.

In the terrible winter which followed, twenty out of the twenty-eight men died from cold and disease. The Frenchmen, coming from a mild climate like that of France, were illy prepared to face a Canadian winter. Instead of a real colony, this was after all but a fur-trading post, and so it remained for a quarter of a century, during which time the population never numbered over one hundred persons.

Champlain was not satisfied in keeping a few Frenchmen in order and bartering trinkets and tools for Indian furs. His dream was of a New France. He wanted to see the great region of mighty rivers and inland seas developed and made full of happy homes and farms, to the enrichment of his sovereign and country. He had a king worth serving, Henry IV., who had not yet been pierced by the dagger of the assassin Ravaillac. When Champlain asked the Indians near Quebec to pilot him on his explorations, they declared themselves quite willing to do so, but only on the condition that he should help them and fight for them, if attacked by the Iroquois. Perhaps Champlain's brain was too busy with the idea of exploration to consider fully the effect of taking sides in Indian warfare. On the other hand, perhaps, he deliberately purposed to make the Algonquins his allies and the Iroquois his enemies.

In the centuries before the red man had possessed the guns and powder of Europeans, his warfare and his industries were quite different from those of later days. His ancient weapons were bows, arrows, and spears. Besides shooting or hurling missiles, he wore armor usually made of bark

or hide. While ever ready for ambuscade and surprise, his frequent method of fighting was by bands
in the open field; or, at least, much more so than
in later times, when he could get a gun and fire
from behind a tree. With the introduction of mus-
kets, the old methods of fighting in mass on open
grounds passed away, though his cunning tricks
and ambuscades, which are very ancient, have never
been given up.

When the summer was well opened in 1609, and
while Henry Hudson in his Dutch ship was sailing
toward the Hudson River, to get within less than
a hundred miles of Champlain and his party, the
three Frenchmen having arquebuses accompanied
the sixty Indians. These were allied Algonquin
and Huron warriors in birch-bark canoes, armed
with flint-headed arrows and spears, and equipped
with bark and skin armor. They moved up the St.
Lawrence River, and entering the river Richelieu
went southward along its western shore and, by the
lake which now bears Champlain's name, into the
territory of New York. Paddling deliberately and
warily past the sites of Rouse's Point, Plattsburg,
and Port Henry, the Algonquins kept ever on the
lookout for their unsleeping enemy, the Iroquois.
In the event of a battle, the allied Indians felt sure
that with the three white men and their firearms
they would surely win the victory.

The human beasts of prey were not disappointed. About two hundred Iroquois from the Mohawk tribe had come up from the region of Schenectady, and were lying in wait at Ticonderoga, hoping that some party of their northern enemies would be coming down on the warpath. It was on the evening of the 29th of July, 1609, that the canoes of the southerners were discovered, but battle was postponed until the next morning. Then both parties being ready and eager, Champlain, dressed in his helmet and jacket of steel, with stout leather trousers and greaves, wearing his sword in his belt, put himself at the head of the Algonquins, and moved out to the attack. He directed his two Frenchmen to go into the woods in order to take the Mohawks in the flank. He had loaded his gun with two balls. When within arrow range he fired, killing two chiefs and wounding another Iroquois. About the same time the two Frenchmen opened fire, while the Canadian savages sent showers of arrows.

All this was so new and strange to the Mohawks, that they probably thought the gods had come to fight with their enemies against them. They saw men holding at their shoulders what seemed to be sticks sending out lightning and thunder. Then, without any apparent cause, for no arrows or spears were visible, they beheld their bravest companions lying dead and wounded. All this so demoralized

them that when the enemies screeched out their
yell of victory, the Mohawks retreated in panic.
They left canoes, bows and arrows, and everything behind, and took to the woods, but not before
ten of their number had been seized as prisoners.
Hardly able to restrain their joy, the savages from
Canada gathered up the spoil, and after tying
their captives, enjoyed the usual dances. Like cats,
they were happy at the idea of having prey to
torment.

Then they turned back and northward down the
lake, stopping every once in a while to cook their
food. They used hot coals and other means of
inflicting pain, in order to make the prisoners of
war suffer as horribly as possible. Indeed, their
refinement of torture seemed more suitable to the
Inquisition than to rude savagery. Champlain tried
to dissuade them, but to the savage such customs
formed part of his nature and religion, and an Indian
would no more change them than the Pope would
alter a church doctrine without a council.

In his exultation at beating the Mohawks, Champlain was quite ready to return at once to France;
and this he did, arriving on the 13th of October.
He told the King how he had discovered and surveyed nearly the whole length of the beautiful
island-studded lake that lies between the Adirondacks and the Green Mountains, all of which

domain he had, by the right of discovery, added to
the realm governed by the House of Bourbon.

In 1611 and 1612, Champlain visited France to
report progress. In 1614, he explored the Ottawa
River. In 1615, he built a chapel at Quebec, and
gave it in charge of missionaries whom he had per-
suaded to come over to New France. From this
time forth, the black-robed friars and fathers become
prominent figures in the annals of American exploration and history.

Although Champlain never saw the Great Lakes,
about which the Indians told him, and which he so
earnestly longed to be the first white man to look
upon, yet his life was one of singular adventure.
He crossed the Atlantic several times. With his
Algonquin allies, he commanded in a second battle
on Lake Champlain, in which the Iroquois were
again beaten. In 1615, he made a journey of nearly
two thousand miles, on foot and in canoe, into
central New York, going by way of the Ottawa
River and Lakes Huron and Ontario. The object
of the host of allied Indians, which he accompanied,
was to assault the great six-sided fort of the Iroquois built near Lake Onondaga. This large war
expedition was a failure, and Champlain was
wounded. The disappointed army of savages,
made up from many Canadian tribes, recrossed
Lake Ontario. While the red men hunted deer,

Champlain studied the country and the native inhabitants.

Champlain must be ranked in the first class of American explorers. He had carried the lilied banners of France far into the territory of what are now the provinces of Ontario, Quebec, and Montreal in the Dominion of Canada and the Empire State of New York, as well as along the Atlantic coast from Labrador to Cape Cod. When he began his work of examining new lands and waters, there was no European settlement in eastern North America between Greenland and Mexico, and no exploration of a scientific character had yet been done between Hudson's and Chesapeake Bay. It is true that navigators had sailed along the coast and noticed the headlands and great bays, and even the Englishmen Gosnold and Pring had touched upon the shores, but Champlain was their first real explorer. He surveyed nearly a thousand miles of seacoast, and his maps were of immense value. These, besides being pretty fair representations of the land and water visited, have on them accurate and properly located drawings of the fish, animals, vegetables, and trees. Champlain's descriptions of the Indians of the United States and Canada, before they were influenced by the white man, are not only the first, but they are of the highest value.

On Christmas Day, 1635, Champlain, in the little

fort on the rocky heights of Quebec, breathed his last. For thirty-two years he had devoted himself with heroic constancy to plant the flag of France in America, and to increase the knowledge of the world concerning northeastern North America. The work did not cease with him, but was carried on by two very different classes of men, the Jesuit fathers and the wood-rangers.

The former, ministers of religion, educated, refined, consecrated, noble, self-denying men, have left behind them records of priceless value. From 1632, the black-robed friars of the Society of Jesus — the Salvation Army of that day — sent home to their general accounts of their missionary work, including their travels. These writings were edited with care and published in Paris. For sixty-one years from 1632 until 1693, when Frontenac stopped the reports from Canada, a duodecimo volume of " Relations," well printed and bound in vellum, dropped annually from the printing-press of Sebastian Cramoisy in Paris. These were reprinted in Italy. Read at Court and by noblemen and people interested in religion and patriotism, these little volumes were awaited as eagerly as to-day we look for the morning journal, or the story-paper or magazine in which is a serial "to be continued." Their authors travelled on foot or travailed in spirit in Canada or Louisiana. To-day these volumes are invaluable as a storehouse of material for the historian, for much of what we know was made possible by the Jesuits.

The French wood-rangers, on the contrary, did not, as a rule, know how to read or write. They have told no story of their wonderful journeys into the virgin forest, over Indian trails, and on waters never traversed by white men till they paddled their canoes over their surfaces. A large part of American exploration was done honorably by these plain, rough, unlettered men.

Champlain probably never knew what a train of influences he had set in motion by that one shot at Ticonderoga. In reality, by a single act he had made it impossible for the French to keep their foothold in America. He did not know what a powerful confederacy that of the Iroquois was, and that their faithfulness to the Dutch and English would be fatal to French dominion in America. As it was, the Mohawks, within a generation, armed themselves with Dutch guns and powder. When Champlain died, they were able to stop for a while both the fur trade and further French exploration. Champlain's shot drew the boundary line between two civilizations. Without knowing it, he rang the knell of French hopes. In the historian's eyes, his bullet pricked the dream-bubble of New France.

ONE of the most important and striking features of the North American continent is that system of great fresh-water seas or lakes, drained by the St. Lawrence River, which conveys their overflow to the sea. There is nothing else on earth quite like this great reservoir of fresh water in the heart of a continent, unless it be the vast unsalted seas in the interior of Africa which supply the Nile River. Forming part of the northern boundary of the United States, and the seat of the greatest inland water commerce in the world, the names of the first explorers of the Great Lakes ought to be familiar to every American boy.

If we look at that plateau of land west of Lake Superior, we shall find the fountains of the Mississippi, the St. Lawrence, and the Red River, three great streams which water the continent east of the Rocky Mountains. These empty into the Gulf of Mexico, the North Atlantic, and Hudson's Bay, respectively. For ages the Indians had glided down the St. Lawrence River, using it as their chief trade-route, exchanging the red stone pipes, copper, and agate arrow-heads of the far West for the sea-shells, salt, and other articles from the ocean's shore. When Champlain came to Canada and saw the copper and the furs, his imagination was powerfully stirred. In prophetic vision he beheld this great river made the highway of a nobler and richer commerce.

The Frenchmen who survived the climate of Quebec took rather kindly to the Indian ways of life. They soon became very much like their savage allies, in habits, dress, food, and love of the forest and of outdoor life. Tough, alert, and in love with wild adventure, they enjoyed life in a birch-bark canoe, with alternate campings out and voyaging into the lands of the beaver and buffalo. Sitting by the roaring fire at night, under the stars, with the solemn trees for a background and the bright waters mirroring the jewelled skies before them, they loved to sing songs, to tell stories, and to hear the Indians recount the lore of their ancestors and their white comrades narrate their experiences. The legends of the red men were ever fascinating to those white men of the woods. Even before the death of Champlain, Brulé had penetrated the region west of Lake Huron. Another voyageur in 1634 paddled through Mackinaw Strait and discovered Lake Michigan.

For nearly twenty years after Champlain's death, in 1635, all French exploration and even the fur trade ceased on account of the Iroquois scourge. Having possessed themselves of guns and powder from the Dutch, the savage men of the Long House in New Netherland were able to fill almost the whole continent with terror. The storehouses at Quebec and the trading stations were empty. The Algonquin Indians scarcely dared to go out beyond their fortified villages, to hunt in the woods, for fear of the musketry of the Iroquois. Not until 1654, when peace between the French and the Five Nations was made, do we find that either the fur trade or exploration was revived.

Then, the way being clear, two Frenchmen, Chouart and Radisson, went out into the Great Lake region and pushed on beyond Lake Superior and wintered with the Sioux Indians among the thousand lakes of Minnesota,—the region of sky-tinted waters. They heard of a great stream, as grand as the St. Lawrence, called the Father of Waters. When these men arrived at Quebec in midsummer of 1660, with three hundred Indians and a fleet of sixty canoes ladened with finest furs, there was great rejoicing in the little colony. All the white settlers in New France were mightily stirred by the stories of those wonderful lands so rich in bison, beaver, sable, and ermine, and of strange Indians whose speech and customs were so different from those of the Hurons and the Algonquins.

From that time on, various parties of adventurous fur traders penetrated into Wisconsin, and some of them probably got as far as the Mississippi. Among many big enemies, the little mosquito, no larger than an interrogation point, proved one of the most annoying obstacles to exploration.

A new governor, Talon, arrived in 1665. He began his work so eagerly that many hoped the white banners of France would soon float in the far West. During the summer his deputy, St. Lusson, with Louis Joliet, raised the French flag at Sault Ste. Marie and took possession of the Lake Superior region, while Courcelles went exploring in person, through woods and waters, finding no enemies worse than mosquitoes. He established a fur-trading post on Lake Ontario, hoping thus to draw away the Iroquois from bartering their furs at Albany.

The copper mines of Lake Superior were still unvisited by any white man, but in 1669, Louis Joliet, an active and lively wilderness-rover, appears on the scene. This man, after many adventures, was commissioned by Governor Frontenac, who arrived in 1672, to explore the Father of Waters. Joliet had for his companions the noble Father Marquette and five fellow wood-rangers ready for new adventures. Joliet spent the winter of 1672 in catechising all the Indians he could meet who had ever been on the great river.

On May 17, 1673, he and his companions began a canoe voyage, going up the Fox River. They pulled out their boats at what is Portage City and put them on their backs. Then, like snails that carry their own houses, they walked two miles and, reaching the Wisconsin River, loaded again and dropped down the stream. After one month from their start, on June 17, the high bluffs of the Mississippi rose before them. They paddled down past the Ohio, Missouri, and Arkansas affluents. Satisfying himself that this great stream flows into the Gulf of Mexico and not into the Pacific, Joliet returned by way of the Illinois River, passing by the site of Chicago up Lake Michigan to Green Bay and thence to Quebec.

Joliet took many notes, but unfortunately he lost his manuscripts when in sight of home, and but fifteen minutes before he landed, by the sinking of a canoe in the river. Nevertheless, he prepared a map and a narrative from memory. He had not found a waterway to the Pacific Ocean, but he had shown that by making but two portages

T

between the mouth of the St. Lawrence and the
Gulf of Mexico, one could traverse all New France
in a canoe. Joliet wanted to go again, but he was
never able to get into the Mississippi valley; for
La Salle, jealous of all intruders into his chosen
grounds, had him kept out of this region. Joliet
was rewarded by being appointed royal hydrogra-
pher and was given the island of Anticosti.

Marquette, after whom a city has been named,
won the confidence of the Indians. He was a good
type of those Jesuit missionaries who were tireless
travellers, fond of exploration and of the new and
wonderful life in the new continent. He had established missions at Mackinaw, Sault Ste. Marie,
and Green Bay. Some of these consecrated men
went from tribe to tribe, carrying on their backs
little portable altars, with breviary, candles, and the
most necessary things for the peculiar services of
the Roman form of Christianity. Their vehicle
was the birch-bark canoe, which carried them when
they were on the water, and which they carried
when they were on land.

Time and space would fail to tell of all the
French explorers DuLhut, Hennepin, Tonti, and a
host of others, who took part in making known the
Great Lake region, the headwaters of the Mississippi, and the heart of British America. Perhaps
like all great works that are evolutions, rather than

inventions, — printing, gunpowder, the steam engine, the telegraph, the landscape of England, an ocean steamer, — the best part of the French, Spanish, Dutch, and British exploration of this continent has been the work of unknown men. The "Great Unnamed" of history, as in holy scripture, are more numerous than those of name and fame.

The greatest figure in the French exploration of America, looming up above all others, is that of Robert Cavelier la Salle. His first and last idea was to make France great. His consuming ambition was reënforced by a magnificent physique, a powerful brain, and an active will. He would serve king and country, first by finding the route to China through French-American dominions, and next by extending New France until it should cover all the North American continent west of the Alleghanies. Arriving in Montreal in 1666, he began immediately to study the Indian dialects and made wonderful progress.

After exploring the forests of northern Canada, he made up his mind that no road to the riches of China and Japan could be found in that direction. His astrolabe, which he lost in the Canadian woods, was picked up a few years ago, after a burial of two centuries; even as one of his axes was recently found in a tree growing near the Mississippi River.

Nor are these the only relics of the man who cut his name so deeply in American history.

A band of the Seneca Indians from the region of southwestern New York visited his little settlement near Montreal and told him of waters that rose in their country, but which flowed into the salt sea, after one had paddled in drinkable water for many months. La Salle immediately began to think that this stream must empty into the Vermilion Sea, or Gulf of California. If so, could he not make his path direct to the Oriental spice lands, besides trading with the Indians and getting rich along the way? This was in 1668-69. His imagination fired, he started out at once. Going up the great ocean river of the St. Lawrence, he explored Lake Ontario and the St. Louis or Ohio River. He also got into the Illinois or some other affluent of the Mississippi, possibly even reaching the main stream, before Joliet and Marquette. Of this we are not certain, but La Salle was the discoverer of the Ohio and the Illinois rivers.

There are two years of La Salle's life shrouded in mystery, during which, it is said, some of his men refused to follow him. They came back to the land near the rapids, nine miles above Montreal, and the people in derision nicknamed the place and the water here "La Chine," or China. In

our day, it is one of the delights of Canadian travel
to shoot the Lachine rapids in a steamer.

La Salle went back to France in 1674 and was
there made a nobleman. Receiving the approval
of the King, he started again to America to make
his great exploration. He gained as a companion,
Henri de Tonti, an Italian of remarkable ability,
whose father's name is still preserved in the Ton-
tine system of life insurance. Tonti's hand had
been lost in the wars, but the surgeons had replaced
the flesh and nerves by a mass of iron which served
its owner handsomely, not only to pull and lift
things, but also to rap the skulls of the savages
when they were stupid or disobedient. Tonti was
a brave and faithful helper of La Salle, and did much
toward making his explorations successful and in
opening the Great West to France. His name
deserves higher honor than it has yet received.

La Salle built a ship near Niagara, on Lake Erie,
the waters of which had never before mirrored a
sail, having floated only canoes. In the *Griffin*,
as this " canoe with wings " was called, he sailed to
Mackinaw and sent back the ship for supplies.
Then with his companions he paddled to near the
southeast corner of Lake Michigan, where at St.
Joseph's River they built a fort. Crossing the country to the headwaters of the Kankakee, which flows
into the Illinois, they floated down the stream, pass-

ing over Marquette's route. At Utica they found corn, and below Peoria Lake wigwams, with Indians, who gave news from both north and south.

La Salle, bitterly disappointed at not being promptly reënforced with supplies, built a stockade called Crevecour, or Broken Heart, near Peoria. Then he began the building of another ship of forty tons. Still the supplies had not come, and what should he do? He could not think of going to the Gulf of Mexico, much less to China, without materials for barter and many other things necessary. The great-hearted leader actually resolved to walk all the way back to Canada, in the depth of winter, to get what he wanted. Over ice and snow, mud and thickets, flood and field, he made the thousand-mile passage in sixty-five days.

While he was away, Father Hennepin started out to make explorations on his own account. He met with wonderful adventures, seeing and describing for the first time the Falls of St. Anthony and passing over the sites of Minneapolis and St. Paul. Hennepin had already seen and described the Falls of Niagara. Hennepin is the harlequin of French exploration, and either he or his editor has made books which make the historian laugh, because of their caricatures of fact and truth.

While in Canada La Salle heard that his men had mutinied and scattered. He at once made the

journey back to the fort of the Broken Heart. He
passed through the Illinois country to find black-
ened ruins where there had been large villages of
Indians. These had been attacked and slaughtered
by the fierce Iroquois from New York, now so terrible with their guns. He found the fort in ruins, but
he passed down to the mouth of the Illinois River,
and saw the Mississippi. He then returned to Fort
Miami on the St. Joseph's River.

No obstacles could daunt this heroic soul. Nature,
and man both white and red, seemed against him.
He resolved to band together the western tribes
against the Iroquois, and in 1681 came back to
Illinois and formed the league. This was an en-
largement of Champlain's policy, as Sir William
Johnson's was of Van Curler's. Then he found
Tonti and returned to Canada.

Having secured new supplies, he once more, in
the autumn of 1681, faced westward. With sleds
and canoes his party of fifty-four persons, civilized
and savage, crossed the portage at Chicago. Now
on runners, and now afloat, they worked their way
down the Illinois River. On the 6th of February,
1682, the whole party entered the ice-blocked Mississippi. He named the river after Colbert, the great
finance minister of Louis XIV. Waiting a week
for the ice to clear away, they made their way southward to summer climes.

At the Chickasaw Bluffs, they drove in some palisades, and called it Fort Prudhomme after the officer left in charge. At the mouth of the Arkansas, a three days' conference was held with the savages, and then on the 14th day of March, 1682, in the name of Louis XIV., King of France, followed the formal ceremony of taking possession of the heart of the continent. Smoking the calumet of peace with the Natchez Indians, visiting other tribes at various points, planting crosses on the shores and bluffs, passing the mouths of the rivers and the site of cities since famous, they kept on, until on April 6 the great lonely flood divided into three channels, in each of which went one section of the party commanded by La Salle, Tonti, and d'Antray, respectively. Reaching the salt air and water, they again united on land near the mouth, having spent nine weeks on the voyage down this wonderful stream.

Landing, La Salle erected a cross and also a post, on which he fastened a metal plate bearing the royal shield resplendent with three fleur-de-lis or lily-heads, the arms of the Bourbon House of France. In the ground was buried one of those many leaden plates which La Salle deposited at various points between Lake Ontario and the Gulf of Mexico, and of which some have been found in our times, on which were engraved, " Louis, the

Great, reigns." His French companions and Indian canoe men fired off their guns and shouted "Vive le roi." In the name of the King of France, Louis XIV., he took possession of the whole territory drained by the Mississippi and its tributaries — about as large as one-third of Europe. To all this great region, unmeasured and unexplored, he gave the name of Louisiana, in honor of Louis XIV. Then the grand old Latin hymn Vexilla Regis, "Forward — let the banners of the King advance," was sung, and another cheer for the King ended the ceremony.

In explorations, La Salle had trodden the soil, threaded the waters, or passed through or alongside of probably a dozen great states of our American Union. In his claim, he took possession of the seas, harbors, ports, bays, adjacent straits, and all the nations, peoples, provinces, cities, towns, villages, mines, minerals, fisheries, streams, and rivers "upon the assurance he had had" (by signs and grimaces chiefly, not a word of the French or Mississippi Indians' language being mutually understood) that La Salle and these Frenchmen were "the first Europeans who have descended or ascended the said river" Colbert. He was particular to state that his possession had been "acquired by the consent of the nations dwelling therein." To-day we see how much the Mississippi had been al-

ready discovered by Cabeza de Vaca, de Soto, Joliet,
and very probably by others before La Salle.

The rest of the story of New France in America
belongs to the romance of colonization and of conquest. We need not here tell of the tragic death
of La Salle, or the foundation of New Orleans and
Mobile and their history. The French founded on
this continent "a vast but transient empire" which
is now a memory. Of the sixty forts which they
built between Canada and Mexico, many are now
the sites of American cities. The missions to the
Indians failed with the failure of New France.

Thus, while the English did next to nothing
toward exploring the continent, still holding only
their first settlements on the Atlantic coast, France
was making known to the world the wonders and
riches of the interior continent. It seemed to be
the design of Providence to let two Latin peoples
do the work of opening this country, in order that
other tribes of the great Aryan race should come
in to possess and colonize.

CHAPTER XXVII.

IN the long struggle between the French and English for the possession of the best portion of
North America, the English people had the advantage. They held the coast and could easily be
helped and reënforced from the mother-country.
The colonists were protected on the north and west
by their allies of the Iroquois confederacy. Best
of all, with English ideas and representative government, the people in the thirteen colonies were
rooted in the soil. They were farmers and made
homes, instead of being, as the French for the most
part were, fur-traders, hunters, soldiers, and priests.
Their organization was civil, that of the French
military. During the eighteenth century, not only
New France but much of New Spain disappeared
from the area now covered by the United States.

Of all the mighty domain over which the lilies
of the House of Bourbon had floated, only two little
islands off Newfoundland remained. These were
allowed for the benefit of French fishermen. When,

during our Revolutionary War, King Louis XVI. and his able minister Count Vergennes lent our fathers aid in ships and sailors, officers, soldiers, and money, it was part of their scheme of European politics. They hoped to get back Canada. Washington, John Adams, and Congress saw their purpose, and preferring English to French neighbors in the north, the campaign was made at Yorktown, and not at Quebec, as the French had desired.

With the fall of New France, the eastern portion of New Spain fell also under Anglo-Saxon sway. Florida was given up to England after a Spanish possession of over two hundred and fifty years. Spain reaccepted Cuba in place of Florida and also her claims in the Pacific coast region of Vancouver Island and the north, in what is now British America.

Very little had been done to explore the land of oranges and magnolias. But soon after Spain had made cession of the territory once named by Ponce de Leon, a Dutch officer named Romaine, a skilful engineer, began the exploration and survey of the country, while Vancouver was sent to the Pacific. Romaine spent some years learning about the human beings and inhabitants of our most southern peninsular state. He wrote the first book in English, and still one of the most important, about Florida.

When the Revolutionary War broke out, Romaine left the service of Great Britain and entered that of the United States. Under Washington's orders he built forts at West Point. He also composed a very valuable historical work which showed that the American revolution was justified, and that the Americans were but following out the precedents already given in the Dutch war of independence against Spain, from 1568 to 1648.

The ground east of the Mississippi was now cleared of rival and hostile forces and the way made open for the union of all English colonies.

In Florida the Spaniards had penetrated the country only a little and had but very slightly developed its resources. They had made slaves of the Indians, but they had also sent many zealous missionaries among them, not a few of whom lost their lives. Negro slavery was begun in 1687. Settlements were made at Pensacola and a few other places. The Spaniards also introduced horses and cattle and oranges. When English settlers came into the new country they found the soil wonderfully fertile, which fact the Spaniards do not seem to have known. In 1783, Florida was again ceded back to Spain, — much to the disgust and loss of the English people living there. It was not until 1822 that the United States flag was hoisted over

Florida, and it became the permanent possession of the Union.

The latter half of the eighteenth century was a famous one in the annals of exploration. Captain James Cook, who, as master of a sloop, had taken part in the capture of Quebec, observed in 1768 at Tahiti in the South Pacific the transit of Venus, which the Dutch-American astronomer Rittenhouse also observed at Philadelphia. Cook also visited New Zealand and explored the coast of New South Wales. In 1772, he sailed again with two ships, hoping to discover the Terra Australis, which was supposed to be a continent in the southern seas. Although he circumnavigated the globe, losing only one man and discovering New Caledonia, he did not find the imaginary continent, which must be classed with Antilia and the supposed lost continent of Atlantis.

There was another transit of Venus over the sun's disc on the 9th of December, 1774, the elements for which were calculated by our own Rittenhouse. The platform used by the astronomers stood in Independence Square in Philadelphia and was used during July, 1776, for the reading of the Declaration of Independence, which showed a new-born political star moving across the disc of history.

In 1776, Cook sailed to explore Behring Strait. He discovered the Hawaii Islands, which were named after the Earl of Sandwich, who also gave his name to stratified refreshments. Cook was killed by the natives, but his lieutenant George Vancouver was ordered to follow up Cook's work.

It was a grand day for Vancouver, who sailed on April 1, 1791. Even the name of his ship, the *Discovery*, showed how interested in exploration the British people and government had become. Among other officers with him were Lieutenant Puget, whose name is left on the great sound in our far northwest, and Broughton, after whom the great bay in Korea is named. Vancouver explored the Pacific coast from the thirtieth degree of north latitude to Cook's Inlet. He entered the waterways to see if the arm of the sea, named by Juan de Fuca nearly two centuries before, was only a strait, yet hoping to find a passage to the Great Lakes in British America. Vancouver's surveys were made with minute care. This illustrious officer is fitly remembered by the island which bears his name, whence noble steamers ply to Japan.

In 1785, La Perouse the French explorer extended the bounds of our geographical knowledge by exploring the northern Pacific coasts of America and Asia. He did not find the Northwest Passage. Though he and his companions lost their lives by wreck on a coral reef, he has left his name on the straits between Saghalien and Siberia.

While the romance of discovery was being slowly written all over the earth by the brave men of Europe, and while their ships, like shuttles wove, as in tapestry, bright pictures of the triumph of science, the native American did his share of work also.

In the eighteenth century there steps into history a new figure. It is that of the explorer born on the soil. He realizes that there is a struggle going on between the great Powers of Europe for the possession of this continent. New Netherland and New Sweden are no longer on the map. The question, whether he is to live in New Spain, New France, or New England, is still uncertain, though the English-speaking colonists believe it is going to be a New England; or, better, a new Europe. The Indian is of a great deal of importance as a political factor, and each Power is trying to get the red man as an ally and friend. The Spaniards do not show much tendency to advance further northward, but the Frenchmen seem determined to press up from Louisiana, and down from Canada, and to build a fence to keep back the Englishmen from crossing the Alleghany. In this they only partially succeed, for New England holds her own along the coast, being easily and quickly reënforced on the ocean from the mother country; while in New York and Pennsylvania, the Dutch and Germans toughly and perseveringly maintain their ground, powerfully aided by the Iroquois confederacy; for Sir William Johnson, following up Van Curler's policy, by his skill and genius, keeps the Six Nations loyal to the British crown. In the South the new wealth from tobacco, cotton, rice, indigo, slave labor, and the genius and enterprise of the English colonists, so nobly reënforced by the sterling qualities of the men of Huguenot and German stock, manifested both in defence and offence, keep the Spaniards from making further advancements.

At such a time, appears the native-born American frontiersman, explorer, Indian fighter, soldier, pioneer, and commonwealth builder. After him bands of pioneers press forward from Virginia and the Carolinas in Kentucky and Tennessee.

The pathfinder in this region is Daniel Boone, — one of that splendid Pennsylvania German stock, which has furnished so much good blood to the country. Though there were other American pathfinders in the eighteenth century, we may take this man as the typical explorer of his age. As early as 1750, Dr. Thomas Walker in behalf of the Loyal Company, and Captain Christopher Gist in behalf of the Ohio Company, passed through Kentucky in search of fertile lands. Before they could locate their claims and settle colonists, the two

U

wars, the French and Indian, and the Revolutionary came on to disturb their plans.

Daniel Boone was born in Bucks County, Pennsylvania, February 11, 1735. He went with other Germans down into North Carolina, where he married. In 1769, with five other young men he penetrated a region south of the Ohio, then uninhabited by white men and covered with virgin forests. Like the Adirondack debatable land, between the Hurons and the Iroquois in northern New York, Kentucky was to the Indians "the dark and bloody ground." Boone and his companions made known the region now covered by Kentucky and Tennessee, and began replenishing it and subduing it for the white race.

In person and ideas, Daniel Boone was a very different character from the first white men who saw the land in 1541. The Spaniards under de Soto, in armor, with swords and spears and clumsy guns that were scarcely anything more than rude hand-cannons, touched Tennessee, where Memphis now stands. Over a century passed, and then the French, led by La Salle, came in Canadian dress, but with the banners and symbols of the Bourbons, and the emblems of a state or political church. Daniel Boone was dressed in hunting shirt, buckskin trousers and moccasins, with coon-skin cap. His gun was a flint-lock rifle. He had not, indeed, the splendid breech-loading rifle of to-day, with its almost mathematically perfect grooving, finely adjusted sights, and waterproof metallic cartridges; yet his was a weapon of unerring power in the hands of a quick and keen-eyed sharp-shooter like himself. The Swiss of Pennsylvania brought the rifle to America; but Kentucky was the ground on which it was developed. Boone's explorations opened the country to settlers, whose sons took part in the battle of King's Mountain in the war of the Revolution. He died on his farm in Missouri, in 1820.

George Rogers Clark was another typical American frontiersman, who knew how to explore and survey, keep back the Indians, and pave the way for new commonwealths. He settled in Kentucky, weakened the power of the Shawnees, secured Illinois from the French, and wrested from the hostile Indians and British the posts at Kaskaskia and Vincennes. He thus enabled the American commissioners, at the Peace Convention in 1783, to fix the western boundary of the United States at the Mississippi River instead of the Alleghany Mountains.

In 1803, under President Jefferson, the United States government purchased from France and Napoleon Bonaparte the whole region between the Mississippi River and the Rocky Mountains, all that was left, but still a mighty domain and the best part, of New France. The price paid was fifteen millions of dollars. Neither Napoleon, nor Jefferson, nor any one else knew in detail very much about the newly bought region. So the next year the chief executive, Jefferson, sent out two competent men to report upon the new territory.

CHAPTER XXVIII.

THE nineteenth-century explorer who now appears in view is of two different types. One
is the frontiersman, rifleman, trapper, and hunter.
Individually, or associated in small parties, he lives
near or just beyond the border of civilization, seeking game and furs, leading parties of emigrants to
their newly bought lands, or accompanying surveyors who go to measure the wilderness and locate
claims. He is a self-reliant, alert, and fearless person, who has learned a great deal from the Indians,
their resources in war and peace, their tricks and
ways; but who, by means of superior intelligence
and finer race-qualities, beats them on their own
ground. Often he is as vindictive and cruel as he
is rough and hardy; but whether as glorified and
idealized by Cooper and the romancers, or as actual
trangressor who falls into the clutch of army officer
or magistrate, he possesses a fair balance of virtues
and vices. Often he is kind and helpful, as generous and as chivalrous as the knights who dressed in

silk and iron. Certainly he aids powerfully in the making of the United States.

In the American frontiersman, there was no display of flaming banners or shining armor; no dazzle of uniforms or emblems; none of the ideas of a state church, of feudalism, of loyalty to king or pope, such as ruled the mind of his Spanish or French predecessors. He was in many respects just as much of a romantic figure, as truly a knight and protector of the weak and innocent, as strong a believer in the destiny of his race, as any of the cavaliers that had entered history before him. Very few of his kind now remain within the United States. With the banishing of the buffaloes, with the coming in of railways and telegraphs he, like the Indians, has dropped out of society, out of politics, and out of use. He is no longer a part of the necessities and machinery of modern civilization.

The other kind of explorer who has done so much to open the Great West which was sold by Napoleon and bought by Jefferson, and to make straight the paths of civilization and Christianity, is the uniformed United States military officer. Brave as a soldier, an explorer, and a pathfinder, he has been none the less a patriot and benefactor because he is a paid fighter. The American regular army officer is a noble figure in the romance of discovery. The whole vast space from the Gulf of Mexico and Old

California to Puget Sound and between the Rocky Mountains and the Pacific Ocean has been changed from New Spain into states and territories of the American Union. The work of examining and pioneering this region has been all done during this century by the civil and military commissioners, explorers, and surveyors, both topographical and geological. These have looked upon, measured, and appraised in detail the western half of the continent; while the sailors and naval officers have sounded, charted, and surveyed the ocean and shores.

These servants of the United States government have told us the past history of the region west of the Father of Waters, reconstructing for us its wonderful marine and animal life. We have learned that a large portion of our western territory is an old ocean bed with islands rising out here and there, in the present form of plateaus and mountains. There are also cañons, parks, forests, lakes, waterfalls, and unique wonders above and beneath the soil that surprise the world. By the vitalizing touch of imagination, as we stand within the National Museum at Washington, we see living again the strange and wonderful forms of animal life, that swam, leaped, or flew in earth, air, and sea, before ever a human being looked upon that strange region, so rich and promising, between the Rockies and the rim of the Pacific.

The two explorers appointed by President Jefferson were Captain Meriwether Lewis, private secretary of President Jefferson and formerly of the regular army, and Captain William Clark, brother of the brave soldier who had conquered Indiana and Illinois for the United States during the Revolution. On May 14, 1804, they took boats at the little log-cabin village called St. Louis at the mouth of the Missouri, which they began to ascend. By July 19, 1805, after over a year's boating and carrying, they had gone four hundred leagues. Before them rose the sides of that tremendous cleft in the mountains, where the river breaks through six miles of a rocky wall twelve hundred feet high. This they named the Gates of the Rocky Mountains. The source of the Missouri is in the Madison River, which rises in the Yellowstone National Park. From the fountain to its fall into the Mississippi, it is three thousand miles long.

Reaching the great divide of waters, the party began to travel overland. On the 7th of October, 1805, having come to headwaters flowing in the other direction to the Pacific, they built canoes, and drifted down the river which they saw was even broader and more rapid than the Missouri. One month later, on November 7, they found themselves near the mouth of this great stream, but in a heavy fog. As soon as the sun rent asunder the

veil of moisture, the Pacific Ocean dawned on their
vision. Fourteen years before, Captain Robert
Gray, a Rhode Islander, who was the first man to
carry the American flag around the globe, had discovered this river and named it from his ship, the
Columbia. Thus, indirectly, Christopher Columbus
received recognition even on the Pacific.

The two explorers took the same route back-
ward, and reached St. Louis September 23, 1806.
They had been absent thirty months, and had travelled over eight thousand miles. Their reports of
the wonderful country traversed gave our American people their first clear idea of the vast extent,
the great possibilities of mineral and agricultural
wealth, and the innumerable wonders in the Great
West.

The region of Oregon and Washington was probably the first territory which the United States was
able to claim directly by reason of exploration.
Yet actual occupation and colonization were necessary to possession. It is even probable that,
owing to the discoveries of Sir Francis Drake two
centuries and a half before, analogous to those of
the Cabots on the Atlantic front, Great Britain
would have claimed and controlled this territory,
had it not been for the American missionary Marcus Whitman, who with Dr. Parker was on gospel
service among the Indians.

When young Whitman heard of the proposition of British colonists to begin settlements on territory which is now in the state of Washington, he rode across the country in midwinter to give the news and urge action that would reflect the stars and stripes on the waters of Juan de Fuca. Surviving the awful hardships of that memorable ride, and emerging without scath from storms, floods, and hostile redskins, Whitman succeeded in stirring up the government at Washington to vigorous action. In the following summer, he led a caravan of nine hundred American colonists to that region. With wagons and horses, axes and rifles, they crossed the continent, settled the region, and secured it for the United States. Whitman was afterwards slain by Indians, but Whitman College is his memorial.

Other vast areas were opened to native American explorers in the various tracts ceded to, or purchased by, the United States,— Florida in 1819, the Texas annexation of 1845 and Cession of 1850, the Mexican Cession of 1848, and the Gadsden purchase of 1853. In 1867, Alaska was bought of Russia for seven million dollars. Explorers like Dall, Whymper, and Schwatka have already done much to make this vast region known. Rich in mines, furs, timber, and fish, Alaska also added five hundred and fifty thousand square miles to our territory; brought the frontier of our national domain

within seven hundred miles of Japan's most northern island, and made San Francisco the central city
of the United States. From Eastport in Maine to
Altoo the most westward Aleutian Island, the distance is about six thousand five hundred miles, and
the area of the United States is about three million
six hundred thousand square miles.

Not only in making known the sea-front and inland waterways of the home of the nation by means
of the hydrographic and geodetic surveys, but also
in distant seas, the American government and private enterprise have been ever active. In many
seas and near the poles, ever since we became a
nation, the stars and stripes have been carried by
our brave seamen. The exploring expeditions of
Commodore Charles Wilkes in the Antarctic, and
of Rear-Admiral John Rodgers into the Arctic
seas, the gallant attempts to reach the North Pole
or to rescue brave comrades, from Dr. Kane down
to Lieutenant Peary and the Cornell glacier party,
form a thrilling story in the annals of science, enterprise, and courage.

Thus, our story of the romance of discovery is
finished, so far as relates to the United States, for
comparatively little yet remains that may be called
unknown land within our national domain. In the
older states some portions, like the Everglades of
Florida, are still but little visited, and regions like

the Adirondacks have only been recently opened
or surveyed. In the far West, there are some
areas still comparatively unknown and unoccupied.
Alaska is but little developed. In the main, however, the greater portion of our national territory
has not only been discovered and explored, but its
surface has been measured and mapped.

In many of the states, New Jersey leading all,
and in the territories also, the geological survey
has been carried out to a wonderful degree. The
student, with the aid of imagination, corrected by
science, can see the invisible. He can picture in
his mind the landscapes and water areas during the
various geologic ages. In mental vision, he be-
holds the great monsters sporting again in air,
earth, and sea. He traverses the great forests that
have made our coal. He notes the working of internal forces and climatic agencies which have deposited the elements and their combinations which
in turn have produced ores, soils, forests, grass, sea-
food, and shells. How these have given room and
opportunity to the various tribes of animals and
men to develop, can be discerned in outline. In
the panorama of the earth's history, one sees the
ice-cap covering like a great white sheet the northern half of the United States; watches the boulders,
including Plymouth Rock, as they are transported
from the north, and discerns the processes by

which the great landmarks and headlands have been carved and shaped.

Imagine the coming, the migrations, the distribution of the first human inhabitants that ever gazed upon the glorious scenery of our beautiful land! See some of them happy, well-fed, and comfortable; others desolate, starving, and finally passing away. Behold their works in the mounds! Pick up their relics on old battle and hunting grounds. Note that some of the favored races, like the Zuñi, hold their own for ages against powerful enemies. Others, like the Iroquois, rise into creditable forms of political life and society, with art and commerce and the deposits and bequests on tradition.

Yet all these aboriginal races, even at their highest, were below that line of ink that divides savage race from civilization, — the line of letters. For, except rude methods of counting time and handing down traditions by means of knotted threads, notched sticks, and woven wampum, the Indian had nothing else by which to record and store up knowledge. There was no written history, and life without letters is death. Whether the Indian by himself could have invented an alphabet, we do not know. Sequoyah or George Guess, the maker of the wonderful Cherokee phonetic system, was a half-breed, with a German father and a Cherokee mother.

With this mention of the red man's entrance into the realm of letters, let our Romance of Discovery come to a close. We have seen that the story of the world's revelation is connected with the wanderings of tribes and the migrations of nations. It took men a long time to learn about other lands than that on which they or their fathers had been born. Only in the course of many centuries did they find that the earth was round and so very large. The replenishing of new continents has been the work of Christian peoples. When they first found out about new countries distant and wonderful, the earth seemed very large. Now that they have swift ships, fast railways, and telegraphs, and can go round the globe in a few weeks, meeting their friends and acquaintances in different parts of this planet, the earth seems smaller than it used to be. A commonplace remark is, " How very small the world is, after all."

So it seemed, as I stood on the Grand Stand at the opening of the World's Columbian Exhibition in Chicago, May 1, 1893. Among the vast assemblage gathered in the White City on the shores of Lake Michigan, were men of nearly every nation under heaven. Scores of red Indians, Eskimos, Mexicans, Alaskans, West Indians, and South Americans, mingled with Europeans, Asiatics, Africans,

Australians, and representatives of almost all the nations of the old world.

My seat was but a few feet distant from that of President Cleveland. On the platform were gathered Japanese, Korean, Chinese envoys from the once Far East, but now, to us, the Near West. The descendents of Columbus and the potentates and commissioners from Europe, especially from the nations that had helped to discover or colonize America, had come from beyond the Atlantic.

In front, lay the lake, with silent gondolas and a veiled colossal figure at the end. The flag-staves held only bundles. The fountain-basins were empty. The roof-lines of the great edifices were dull. The sky was overcast.

Prayer to Almighty God, music, an address by the Director-General, preceded the thrilling moment of revelation. Then, the President of the United States advanced to touch an electric button. It was a moment pregnant with surprises.

A crash of sound and a blaze of color followed.

Cannon roared. Steam whistles blew their blasts. Bells rang their peals. The great engine set acres of machinery in motion with buzz and whirr. Huzzas rent the air.

This for the ear!

Most glorious was the revelation of color to the eye. Electric fountains burst into bloom of spray, the golden statute of Columbia unveiled her resplendent form. Aloft on their staves, the sailor's knots burst into a blaze of color and glory, as the flags of Castile and Aragon floated on the breeze, beside the starry banner of the free republic.

So culminated the Romance of Discovery. All due honor to Columbus and to those, also, who went before, or who followed after him!

Laus Deo.

www.ingramcontent.com/pod-product-compliance
Lightning Source LLC
Chambersburg PA
CBHW060547030726
47498CB00005B/1301